Praise for *Clients, Clients, and More Clients*

If "who you know" and making a meaningful connec[tion are a suc]cess factor in business (and it is), I promise you that La[rina Kase's] *Clients, Clients, and More Clients* will have your phone ringing and e-mail box full of people who truly want to do business with you. A savvy, wise, and value-based text allows the reader to learn what few others understand: the Science and Art of Connecting. I've read and reviewed a dozen books on building a solid client base. Most completely miss the target. This book is a handbook to meet, connect with, and build a valuable relationship with just about anyone you want to.

—Kevin Hogan, Psy.D.
Author of *The Science of Influence* and *The Psychology of Persuasion*

This is a remarkable, readable, and instantly practical book packed with leading-edge tips on attracting new clients fast. I loved it! —Dr. Joe Vitale
Author of *The Attractor Factor*

In *Clients, Clients, and More Clients*, Larina Kase shows you how to find and influence prospects so they'll understand the value of your work and readily do business with you. The research-based strategies in this important and engaging book are worth any businessperson's time, close study, and dedicated application. The book is true to its promises.

—Mark Levy
Founder of Levy Innovation and Author of
Accidental Genius: Using Writing to
Generate Your Best Ideas, Insight, and Content

Clients, Clients, and More Clients is a *must*-read for every sales executive, sales manager, and company executive. *Clients* is not your "typical" *how-to* sales guide, as it digs deep into how to change a losing sales strategy into a winning success. Larina uncovers the psychology behind the sales mentality, and breaks the process down, step-by-step; making it crystal clear the direction you'll need to take to achieve long-term success.

—Shawn Jennings Edgington
CIC, CEO, and Founder of Granite Insurance Brokers
Cyber Safety Academy Fundraiser
Author of *The Parent's Guide to Texting, Facebook and Social Media*

Whether you call it the power of psychology or a magnetic personality, the techniques, strategies, and tactics Dr. Larina Kase outlines are exactly what I have used to assist in producing over $20 million in online sales and tens of thousands of customers and raving fans throughout the world in the past five years. It all begins with your ability to communicate and build relationships, and this book gives a step-by-step process on how to get people to know, like, and trust you. With that foundation, the world is limitless and is at your fingertips.

—Tom Beal
Internet Entrepreneur
Founder of MyTransformationSecrets.com

I constantly see business owners waste time, energy, and money on marketing that doesn't pay off. If only they had this book when they opened for business! Larina's expertise in psychology and marketing would have shown them how to make marketing profitable, effective, and fun. This gem of a book should be in the hands (not on the shelf) of every business owner and salesperson responsible for bringing in new business.

—Angela Nielsen
Founder and Creative Director of
One Lily Creative Agency

Larina Kase's book *Clients, Clients, and More Clients: Create an Endless Stream of New Business with the Power of Psychology* is a must-read for any business owners who wants to build their business through referrals and relationship-based selling. As someone who regularly uses and teaches collaborative business-building strategies, I was particularly impressed with her ideas and practical advice on joint-venturing and partnering.

—Kathryn Rose
CEO and Cofounder of Social Buzz Club, the
World's First Online Marketing Collaboration Network

Clients, Clients, and More Clients shares cutting-edge psychology research on how to connect with your clients and customers—the most important thing that business owners and salespeople need to do. We need to leverage our time and energy on marketing that really works—read this book to find out exactly how.

—Sheri McConnell
Millionaire Mompreneuer and Founder of
The Smart Women's Institute of Enterpreneurial Learning

As copresident of a rapidly growing wealth management firm, many of my primary responsibilities require significant people skills. *Clients, Clients, and More Clients* teaches how to address emotional as well as intellectual needs when developing relationships with clients, partners, and coworkers. I have implemented many of the techniques that I learned in this book, and the results have been very favorable. Thank you, Larina, for expanding my thought process and helping my business continue to grow.

—Alan Cohn
Cofounder and Copresident of Sage Financial Group

Anyone who wants to gain new clients needs this book! Dr. Kase deftly combines the neuroscience, social psychology, and art of persuasion to show how you can gain new clients *without* being someone you're not. She shows that recruiting new clients isn't about manipulation or trickery, but rather engaging science to become more of your best self.

—Amy Showalter
Author of *The Underdog Edge: How Everyday People*
Change the Minds of the Powerful . . . and Live to Tell About It

Afraid of wasting your valuable time on marketing efforts that don't get results? Worried about having to sell your soul to sell yourself? Don't worry—just read this book! Larina Kase shows you how to leverage your time and make marketing authentic and enjoyable. The result? More connections, more opportunities, more clients.

—Milana Leshinsky
Author of *Coaching Millions* and
Creator of Recurring Revenue Revolution

In today's busy world, it's quite a challenge to break through the information overload and get recognized. Larina makes it easy to engage and maintain client relationships with her step-by-step guide. I love how she provides action items at the end of each section so you can simply follow the steps to success. This is a great book and a must-have for businesses that enjoy having clients!

—Julie Donley, RN
Author of *Does Change Have to Be So H.A.R.D.?*

This is an incredible book! Larina offers the rare balance we all want: On the one hand she teaches you the fascinating science behind why clients will work with you so your income and quality of life are no longer left to guesswork. On the other hand, she is personable and engaging; you feel that she knows your exact concerns and frustrations and can get you to take right actions to grow your business. Just reading it, I felt as if she was personally coaching me to stand out, reach people, and make a real difference. I will use it as my marketing "bible" and give it out to my clients.

—Sharon Melnick, Ph.D.
President, Horizon Point, Inc.

Once again, Larina's insight into using the power of psychology to maintain an endless stream of clients gives us the nuggets to truly build the business of our dreams. Having experienced firsthand the results of such expertise, I can share that *Clients, Clients, and More Clients* is a must-read book for anyone wanting to maintain a client base with ease and have record-breaking results.

—Sara Canuso
Personal Branding Specialist
President, A Suitable Solution

By reading *Clients, Clients, and More Clients*, you will learn how to leverage the power of psychology to build your brand, grow your business, and live a better life.

—Dan Schawbel
#1 International Bestselling Author of *Me 2.0*
and Founder of Millennial Branding

Today, every organization is in the connection business. In this book—chock-full of ideas at the intersection of marketing and psychology—Larina Kase shows you how to master the art of building relationships that drive new clients.

—David Meerman Scott
Bestselling Author of *Real-Time Marketing & PR*

Larina Kase knows about social proof. You can tell by who she got to endorse the book. But go deeper. There's lots of actionable information in here, and it *will* result in more business.

—Chris Brogan
Coauthor of *Trust Agents*
President of Human Business Works

Most books on psychology and business are heavy on theory and low on practical information. This book is *not* one of them. I highly recommend *Clients, Clients, and More Clients* to anyone who has ever wished for . . . well, more clients. This book is ideal if you've ever wondered how to differentiate yourself from the crowd, how to *really* build relationships that pay off, and how to establish your expertise with ease. This is one book you will thank yourself in the future for!

—Shama Kabani
Author of the bestselling *The Zen of Social Media Marketing*

Larina Kase has done a first-rate job of explicating many crucial elements of human psychology. But it is her instructive advice on how to harness that information profitably that elevates this book's usefulness to great heights.

—Robert B. Cialdini
Author of *Influence: Science and Practice*

Clients, Clients, *and* More Clients

CREATE AN ENDLESS STREAM OF NEW BUSINESS WITH THE POWER OF PSYCHOLOGY

LARINA KASE, Psy.D.

New York   Chicago   San Francisco   Lisbon   London   Madrid   Mexico City
Milan   New Delhi   San Juan   Seoul   Singapore   Sydney   Toronto

1 2 3 4 5 6 7 8 9 0   QFR/QFR   1 6 5 4 3 2 1

ISBN   978-0-07-177075-0
MHID   0-07-177075-5

e-ISBN   978-0-07-177100-9
e-MHID   0-07-177100-X

This publication is designed to provide accurate and authoritative information in regard to the subject matter covered. It is sold with the understanding that neither the author nor the publisher is engaged in rendering legal, accounting, securities trading, or other professional services. If legal advice or other expert assistance is required, the services of a competent professional person should be sought.

> —*From a Declaration of Principles Jointly Adopted by a Committee of the American Bar Association and a Committee of Publishers and Associations*

McGraw-Hill books are available at special quantity discounts to use as premiums and sales promotions or for use in corporate training programs. To contact a representative, please e-mail us at bulksales@mcgraw-hill.com.

This book is printed on acid-free paper.

To my sister Nicole—

*Thank you for putting up with all of my childhood marketing
and sales antics, for being my first loyal customer, and for
investing your valuable quarters in my creative ventures—
I owe you several years of allowance
plus several decades of interest!
You epitomize the concepts in this book
and are an amazing salesperson because you are curious,
gracious, smart, loyal, and caring.
Your clients are lucky to have you, and so am I.*

Contents

Part 1
How Do I Initiate Relationships That Get Results?

Part 2
How Do I Create Meaningful Connections That Last?

Part 3
How Do I Influence People to Refer to Me, Hire Me, and Buy from Me?

Foreword

I LOVE THIS book. If you're in the bookstore and leafing through the pages, stop right now, walk to the counter, and buy it. If you've already bought it and you're deciding whether to read it, what on earth are you waiting for?

What will this book do for you?

Make you popular. True story. Walk into any high school and you'll quickly get a read on the popularity landscape. Kids hang out with other kids on the same level. Preps, punks, goths, freaks, and geeks go about their way in their small cliques. Social jocks and cheerleaders buzz about campus with heaps of admirers. The intellects quietly study together. The too-cool-for-school kids talk trash, trends, and swap iTunes beats. Nonconformists lurk around corners. Band, drama, and choir kids make music and more together.

Who are *you* going to make music with—beautiful business music? The sound of ka-ching, ka-ching that sings the song of inspired clients and money in the bank.

Growing your business, first and foremost, starts with rock solid relationships. The reason you aren't attracting new clients is because they don't know who you are. And you're not yet in their social circle. Expand your circle of influence and you'll instantly be the new cool kid on the block.

Since there's only one of you and thousands of potential business relationships, you might as well take the easy road. Expose the very best of who you are and all that you have to offer.

Open yourself up to a bigger, broader world of new clients drawn to your expertise and appeal.

But wait. Your business isn't going to thrive (or even limp along) by happenstance. Get into the groove. Add new clients to the books. Attract them to you like bees to honey.

How? By understanding the intersection of psychology and practicality revealed in the pages of this book. In fact, this book is the key that will open any door, window, gate, or other metaphorical barrier that gives you access to influential people in your field and a steady stream of inspiring, ideal clients.

Relationships build over time. Consider someone you have hired. When you first met, your relationship didn't go from 0 to 60 in 4.2 seconds. You courted, flirted, and got to know each other. Growing more and more familiar until you reached a level of trust and comfort.

Maybe you heard nice things about this professional from someone sitting at your table. Maybe the chemistry was crackling at your first meeting, and they even called back the very next day! Oh, the magical days of a budding a new relationship.

What are you doing today to meet and court new clients?

New clients don't throw themselves into chilly, untested, sight-unseen waters. Nor do they jump into personal or business relationships without a little getting to know one another. They tiptoe at first. Stand safely at the back of the room. Silently, taking it all in. When they finally feel comfortable, they may open up a little and ask a few questions, revealing more each time. Eventually they trust themselves (and you) enough to invest a little heart, a little soul, and hopefully some hard-earned cash.

Waiting, hoping for this to happen is a recipe for disaster. "Well, maybe everything will just change today and the phone will start ringing." Won't happen. Not today. Not tomorrow. And certainly not the next day.

But *you* can *make it happen.* Even so, building relationships (aka networking) is not something you can force. It's a way of being. The actions that you take, to meet new people and deepen your relationships, stem from this way of being. The result is a life filled with meaningful relationships and a business filled with ideal clients, clients that energize and inspire you and, most important, allow you to do your best work.

Don't let yourself get caught up in a marketing hamster wheel. In fact, Dr. Larina Kase is going to help you off it and ensure you never get back on. You don't need to learn super-secret business tips or execute intense marketing strategies. Instead, read this book, and learn how to deliberately develop deep, personal and professional relationships. One step after another launches a new way for clients to know, love, and hire you.

Only on late-night infomercials are results guaranteed. You, Larina, and I know that the future is uncertain. But we can, if we're serious about our future, create the circumstances that will allow us to navigate to the kind of results that please us. No. Strike that—that make us jump for joy. This book is your map.

Start by embracing the absolutely unequivocal fact that Larina is a loving teacher with an open heart and brilliant mind, offering you, in the pages of this book, a path forward toward a future of your choosing.

I love you very much—not in a weird way, but for standing in the service of others as you stand in the service of your destiny.

Think big—no, bigger than that!

Michael Port

Bucks County, PA
New York Times bestselling author of four books

Acknowledgments

I AM FORTUNATE to have incredible people in my life and am grateful to have this opportunity to acknowledge them.

My parents, Eric and Carol, have supported me no matter what. Back when I was in college and studied psychology, art, *and* business, they never once asked me, "So, what are you going to do with your life?" They knew I would find a way to bring all of my passions together. Similarly, my grandparents Moraima and John's steadfast belief in me has been instrumental.

I would like to thank John for being an amazing husband, father to our children, and support to me and my business. I am grateful to my family, including Nicole, Jamie, Donna, Chuck, Jen, Jim, June, Cesare, Earl, Roger, and Arnelle—I have learned so much from each of you and greatly enjoy our time together.

My literary agent, Rita Rosenkranz, is top in her field, and I am so fortunate to have collaborated with her on several projects now. Likewise, my editor, Donya Dickerson, has the unique ability to position a project to suit the needs of the readers and has been invaluable in the creation of this book. I appreciate the other editors, designers, and team members at McGraw-Hill who have contributed to this book.

Relationships are the cornerstone to success and fun in business. I've loved building joint venture partnerships with incredible people—too many to list here, but you know who you are. And I've been fortunate to receive support from virtual assistants and business managers, including Cindy Greenway, Raven Howard, and Jackie Finch.

I'd like to acknowledge the psychology researchers and authors who have contributed so much to the fields from which I draw—Edna Foa, Robert Cialdini, Sheena Iyengar, Timothy Wilson, Daniel Gilbert, and Kevin Hogan, to name just a few.

And, of course, to my clients. I hope that the people reading this are fortunate enough to work with clients, clients, and more clients as wonderful as you!

Introduction

I WAS 27 YEARS old, fresh out of graduate school, and just getting used to being called "doctor." I had a lot of student loans so I worked part-time as a restaurant server, and when customers would say "Miss," I was tempted to say, "Actually, it's Doctor." Anyway, I was eager to launch my consulting business, but I was stuck. I was intimidated by all of the seasoned coaches and consultants out there. Despite having a background in marketing, I was unsure about how to go about marketing my own business. So I took a step back and asked myself what I knew that could help. A couple of things came to mind: understanding how people think and knowing how to build relationships.

With these things in mind, I somehow got up the courage to approach head honchos in major companies in Philadelphia and ask them to lunch to discuss collaborating. To my surprise, 100 percent of people agreed, and almost three-quarters of them turned into long-term strategic referral partners. Encouraged by the success of these efforts and how much I was enjoying connecting with people, I decided to contact a famous author and suggest that he and I do a joint venture. He was interested, and we ended up doing several projects together. Through networking I met a producer for a major television show and ended up serving as an expert on a program with millions of viewers.

The results of these efforts showed me just how powerful—and how much fun—building business relationships can be. I didn't have anything special other than knowledge of psychology, which I'm eager to share with you so you can achieve results like these. As a salesperson and rainmaker for a company or the owner of a service business, your success rests on your ability to bring in new clients. Your ability to get new clients begins with your ability to connect.

The Art and Science of Connecting

People say, "Timing is everything." While I agree that timing is important, I say, "Connecting is everything."

Your connections determine how someone

- Becomes your client
- Refers to you
- Becomes your fan or loyal follower
- Hires you to speak or train
- Becomes a great joint venture partner
- Becomes a colleague or mentor
- Connects you with others
- Endorses your work and ideas
- Happily pays you what you are worth
- And much, much more

Together we're going to go through a process of discovering how to initiate powerful professional relationships, how to turn these relationships into loyal, trusting ones that will last for a long time, and how to leverage these relationships to increase your business through referrals and joint ventures.

Communications research shows that *what* you say is not as important as *how* you say it. Nonverbal communication, things like your body language and tone of voice, account for approximately 65 percent of the message that is received. Similarly, *what* you do to connect with people (attend networking events, connect on LinkedIn, and so on) is important but not as important as *how* you go about connecting with people.

There is both an art and a science behind how to initiate and maintain business relationships that get bottom-line results. I will share the science with you here. It comes from cutting edge and classic studies in psychology. As a psychologist specializing in cognitive-behavioral theories, I've studied how people think, feel, and behave—the three things you must understand to best connect with people and influence them to take action. In addition to cognitive-behavioral psychology, I draw from research in social psychology and neuroscience to help you understand

- What attracts people and makes them want to do business with you.
- What makes people remember you.
- What deepens connections and makes relationships meaningful.
- What makes people take action and make purchases or referrals.

So that's the science. The art comes from personalizing the science in the way that works best for you and those who you do business with. Sometimes people think of psychology and influence as ways to come across as something you're not. This is the opposite of what's true. Instead, the goal is for you to be *more* of who you are—to select the marketing actions, the people, and the style that best fit with who you are. This is the art.

The Three Most Common Challenges in Relationship Marketing

You know those people who instantly attract and connect with everyone they come into contact with? These people make others feel at ease. They make everyone feel special. They are charismatic and magnetic. *If this is not you, don't worry.* You don't need to do these things to be very successful at building business relationships. If this is you, that is great, you have a natural gift that we can leverage to ensure that your connections lead to real-world business results.

Following are the top three challenges people face in building relationships to build their businesses. Some people mostly struggle with one area. Most of us have some challenges with various aspects of all three. Which of these three areas do you struggle with?

Challenge 1: You do not attract the attention of and initiate relationships with the right people

Perhaps you're shy and approaching people doesn't come naturally to you. Or perhaps you are fearless and go up to anybody but don't stand out enough to make them take notice and want to learn more. Perhaps you aren't sure who to approach or how to go about doing it. I recently conducted an online survey of hundreds of business owners, salespeople, and service professionals whose success depends on their ability to attract new clients via relationships and referrals. When asked about their greatest marketing challenges, people said things like:

- "Identifying the right people to begin a relationship with."
- "Making contact with the right decision makers."
- "Getting people to listen. Getting their attention. Getting past voice mail."
- "It is tough to get the initial meeting. You must differentiate yourself from the other 10 people they may have spoken to that day."

These are the topics we will cover in Part 1, Chapters 1 through 4. You'll discover the psychology behind who to approach, how to get attention and make yourself stand out when you approach them, and how to develop immediate emotional connections.

Challenge 2: You do not follow-up and connect to form trust, an emotional bond, and ongoing relationships

This is the business-card-collection phenomenon. You meet potential business partners, make a positive impression. You and the others involved are excited about the opportunities. But the follow-up is not there. As a result, you fail to build strong alliances and create opportunities to work together. Those who responded to my survey reported challenges such as:

- "Finding the common ground in a relationship that you can build upon."
- "Developing trust on both sides."

- "Balancing the right mix of follow-up and not coming off as pushy."
- "Finding unique ways to stay in touch on an ongoing basis."

We'll cover these topics in Part 2, Chapters 5 through 8, in our discussions of how to build relationships over time by following up and being memorable in ways that add value to others.

Challenge 3: You do not convert relationships into referrals and new clients and customers

Some people do a great job with both challenges 1 and 2. They create a positive first impression and have great keep-in-touch and follow-up. The problem? They have created many new *friends*. They give all their stuff away. They don't get clients, referrals, and actual business from these relationships. They are likeable but don't generate sales. We're talking business relationships, not solely friendships, so there must be a benefit to the bottom line. Business owners, salespeople, and service professionals in my survey reported difficulties such as:

- "Getting referrals back—I am the connector but would like reciprocation."
- "Getting clients to refer me to others."
- "Turning people who love me and my free stuff into buyers."
- "My reluctance to ask for referrals."

Our bottom-line goal is for you to build your business. In Part 3, Chapters 9 through 12, we'll explore four powerful principles that influence action: social proof, reciprocity, simplicity, and influencing decision making.

Being the Best and Taking Action

We will begin our journey together with an understanding that you are passionate about and great at what you do. I will not get into how to be the best possible service provider that you can be—you know more about your profession than I do. You know the continuing education, professional development, supervision, and consultation routes that you can take to enhance your expertise and your client outcomes. *Do these things.* The most important thing you can do is to be the best in the world at what you do.

Here is my formula for marketing success:

Be the best + Have a great marketing strategy
+ Use psychology as you implement your strategy
= Clients, clients, and more clients!

To create your great marketing strategy, I highly recommend reading *Book Yourself Solid* by Michael Port if you haven't already (or rereading it) and choosing from among his seven core self-promotional strategies: networking, direct outreach, referrals, Web strategy, speaking and demonstrating, writing, and keep-in-touch. I am honored to include Michael's foreword in this book because *Book Yourself Solid* and this book go beautifully hand-in-hand.

The social influence tools you're about to learn are powerful. Take that power seriously, and carefully consider how you will use them to benefit your clients and community. Prioritize the ethical standards of your profession and your personal code of ethics. Be sure that you are providing the best possible service to your clients to ensure that you serve each and every one to the best of your ability.

As you know, knowledge is nothing without action. Ultimately our goal is to help people take action—to hire you, refer from you, buy from you. Similarly, *you* will need to take action. To help you put the ideas into action, I include Action Steps. You may get the best results from selecting a few and doing them consistently rather than trying to do everything at once.

You'll find that the more you use the psychology principles we discuss, the better marketing results you'll get. You'll begin to enjoy connecting. You'll feel great about what you have to offer. You'll approach people in the way that they will be curious and interested—the benefits will be clearly mutual. You won't need to sell yourself or be pushy or salesy. You'll exude a natural magnetism and confidence. As I discuss in *The Confident Leader*, confidence results from approaching something challenging in the right way with the right skills and then practicing it as much as possible. You start to get better results, and your confidence will build. Consequently, the focus will shift from quantity to quality. Your marketing efforts will require less time because they will be more powerful. My goal is for you to enjoy the process of building business relationships, and, of course, the impact on your bottom line. Relationships are my favorite part of doing business, and with the ideas you're about to learn, I hope they become your favorite part too!

Are you ready to learn the psychology of how to get clients, clients, and more clients?

Great! Let's begin.

Part 1

How Do I Initiate Relationships That Get Results?

Chapter 1

Make the Right Connections— People Look for Those Who Fill a Need

---

Many a live wire would be a dead one except for his connections.

—WILSON MIZNER

PERHAPS YOU CAN relate to one of my clients, Stacey:

"I know I need to get out and network, but I don't know the right places to go, don't have any time to do it, and don't really want to. I don't really like talking about myself, and I don't want to come across as pushy or needy. Social media networking is fun, but hasn't paid off for me. I don't want to waste my time networking if nothing is going to happen from it."

Like Stacey, you may find it difficult to initiate conversations and begin business relationships. Or you may be a natural networker. Either way, the first critical step is getting in front of the right people.

Why We Don't Get Out and Meet People

We can come up with millions of excuses for why we don't meet people and market our businesses. Two of the most common factors that stop people from going out and pursuing connections are the lack of time and lack of confidence.

Making time to make connections

In an online survey I conducted about the challenges of relationship marketing, hundreds of people responded that they have no time to network, connect, and follow up. I understand the busy lifestyles that we all have and how difficult it can be to make the time. I also believe that we make time for what's important. If we saw substantial payoff in our business, we would make the time. And if others saw substantial benefit in connecting with us, they would make the time to do so.

The great thing about learning the psychological principles we will discuss is that when you use them, your efforts will pay off more quickly and powerfully. You will actually spend less time because what you do will work better. For this reason we will not discuss time management. Rather, commit to putting the ideas you learn here into practice, dedicate enough time, and you will start to see results fairly quickly.

The challenge with all forms of marketing, however, is that results are typically not immediate. You will need to continue to put some time in and do the work before you get an immediate reward. You will see results months and years after you put the time in. I often get e-mails from clients who I worked with in the past telling me how they put the ideas we discussed into practice for six months or so and their businesses and practices took off exponentially. This means that your initial time investment will be substantially higher than your ongoing time investment. Think of this like the principle of inertia—a body at rest stays at rest, and a body in motion stays in motion. It takes a great deal more to get things moving than to keep them moving. Once you put the time and energy in to get things moving, they will begin to pick up speed on their own—and you'll have much more time to do with whatever you'd like.

Building confidence to make connections

In working with hundreds of service business owners, I've found four primary causes for not having confidence to get out and network.

1. **Lack of clarity about exactly what you do and how you help people.** When you do not feel confident about your brand and message, it is difficult if not impossible to want to get out and share it. Without a clear message and a way to grab attention, your fear can be valid because people may not listen or respond as you would like. Often people who lack confidence in their message and unique value become focused on the competition. They see others who do what they do and think that they do not measure up. Remember that we can always find someone better because we are our own worst critics. Do not bother comparing yourself to the "competition." Know that you are unique and different and even if you offer the same services as someone else, you may better benefit particular people because they resonate with *you*. We'll discuss ways to grab attention, engage emotion, and show your credibility in the next three chapters.

2. **Lack of confidence that you will follow up with people.** Networking does take some time. If we believe that we won't follow up with people, we may figure, "Why bother?" This is a good question, and the answer is that you shouldn't bother networking if you will not follow up. There are two primary reasons that you may have difficulty following up. The first reason is a personal lack of organization. Some people, such as those with attention deficit disorder, are naturally less organized and focused. If this is your challenge, you can work on creating systems to help you. These systems include external accountability and support, such as with a coach, assistant, or friend; office organization systems; contact management systems, such as that offered by the Web site Solid.ly; and so on. The second reason is that you aren't sure how to best follow up and deliver ongoing value. We'll go through strategies for effectively following up in the second section of this book.

3. **Lack of confidence that people will take action.** This concern is similar to the previous one. If you are not confident that people will hire you, refer to you, or buy from you, you're likely to figure, "Why bother?" When you learn the strategies in the third part of the book, you will be better able to stimulate action and make your marketing pay off. Once you do this, you will have greater confidence the next time.

4. **Lack of extroversion.** Initiating conversations is more difficult if you are shy. If you're introverted, it may not be particularly comfortable for you to go up to people and start talking. By the way, introversion and public speaking anxiety are not the same thing. Extroverts can also have public speaking anxiety. If you're nervous about speaking in public, find tips on my blog, EndSpeakingAnxiety.com. If you are not necessarily nervous but are on the quiet side, take heart: Extroverts do not always have the advantage. Sometimes extroverts overwhelm people and talk *at* people rather than *to* them. The key really is to be yourself— introverted, extroverted, or in between. When you connect in an authentic way, people respond.

Do any of these sound familiar? If so, don't worry, they do not need to hold you back from initiating relationships.

Why We Don't Get Out and Meet People?

ACTION STEPS

1. **Block time on your calendar.** We can't make changes without devoting time to take action. Ask yourself realistically what time is needed to devote to building relationships and what you can currently do. Even if you can devote only one hour per week at this point, it is better to be realistic and plan how to maximize that hour. Ideally, plan on five to

six hours per week. Block the time on your calendar and use it to work through the exercises in this book and take action. Treat this time as if it were a meeting with the CEO of a major company. Do not let it get bumped in favor of other things.

2. **Commit to reducing procrastination and perfectionism.** I like to say, "Done is better than perfect." If you spend all of your time perfecting your marketing plan, you will not have any time to implement it. Stop thinking and start doing.

3. **If you're shy, be extroverted in an introverted way.** If you're naturally shy, do not see this as a weakness, but rather recognize the strengths. You will need to act a bit extroverted in order to initiate conversations, but do so in the way that best suits your personality and comfort level. You don't need to be overly vivacious, hilarious, or anything else that isn't necessarily you. If you modify your typical approach by 20 percent or so, you will feel authentic to what is natural to you but be flexible to the needs of the situation.

4. **Be a mirror.** Focus on connecting with people by mirroring their energy level and body language. If you're naturally shy, this can be a way to gain more energy by simply reflecting back what you feel from others. You don't need to be a parrot or exact mirror image, but if someone is leaning forward, engaged in the conversation, don't lean back with your feet up. If someone is speaking very quickly with a fairly loud voice and a lot of energy, reflect some of this back. Again, think of modifying your typical style by about 25 percent so that you're in synchrony with the other person. If you modify your approach by 100 percent, you will not feel authentic or comfortable.

5. **Notice the shift in your energy.** As you work through these exercises, you are likely to feel more focused and energized. In turn you will likely be more efficient, achieve greater results, and invest less time. This shift can take minutes, days, weeks, or months. If you've been avoiding building relationships, you may initially find an increase in discomfort and decrease in energy. Stick with it and the shift will happen.

Finding the Right People

Once you've overcome the time and/or confidence concerns that may hold you back from connecting with others, the next step is to determine who you'll meet and how you'll do so.

Figuring out which networking events to attend

There are dozens of online and offline networking events, so we need to be selective about where to invest our time, energy, and money. Here are some questions to ask yourself to evaluate whether a networking event is likely to be worthwhile.

- **Is it convenient?** If it requires an hour of driving each way, four hours of a babysitter, and less time spent with clients or developing your business, it definitely needs to meet the other criteria.
- **Is it expensive?** If you need to join an expensive association to attend, be sure that you speak with a member relations professional about a free trial where you can attend at least one event at no charge to see if it is a good fit for you.
- **Is it packed with potential clients?** If so, then it is likely to be worth checking out.
- **Is it packed with potential referral partners?** If so, then it is definitely worth checking out. Referral partners are one of the best ways to build your business. If you can meet many potential referral partners at a networking event and then follow up with them individually, you have a great situation.
- **Will I stand out as unique?** Many networking situations are with professionals similar to yourself. These professionals are unlikely to be potential referral partners or clients. Attend the event if you are likely to be the only person in your field or one of just a few who each specialize in a distinct area of your field (for example, a divorce attorney, intellectual property attorney, or trusts and estates attorney).

- **Is it easy to meet the attendees in other venues?** If you can easily meet people individually, you might skip the networking piece and jump right to one on one or small group meetings.
- **Is it a place I could speak?** I always recommend trying to be the speaker at a networking event rather than attending. This elevates your platform and puts you in a position of power in which people want to talk with you. We discuss this more in Chapter 4.

Is it better to cast a wide net or keep your network small and personal?

I recently asked this question on my Facebook page (Facebook.com/ MarketingPsych). Most people felt that quality is more important than quantity. This is true because you'll need mutually respectful and beneficial relationships for someone to think of you and refer to you. It can be hard to maintain this type of quality in your relationships if you have too many. Imagine that you had 50 close friends; it would be impossible to keep in touch with and get together with all 50, and eventually your friendships would suffer. I see the optimal quantity as something like Figure 1.1.

Figure 1.1 Optimal Number of Relationships

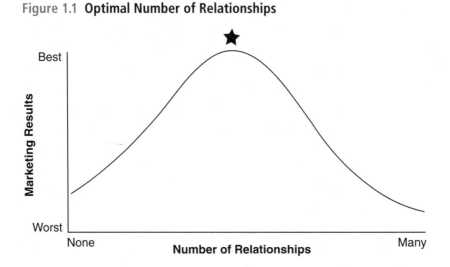

I created this modification of the Yerkes-Dodson Law (which shows the optimal level of anxiety for peak performance) to graphically show how you'll get your best results with the optimal number of connections. Too few and you'll have a timing and numbers issue—enough people won't need you at any one point in time for you to have a thriving business. Too many and you'll be spread thin, and the quality of your relationships will suffer. It may be tempting and ego gratifying to focus on numbers (such as how many friends or followers you have), but in my experience quality is equally if not more important.

One exception to this rule is *influencers*. Influencers are people who have a high degree of influence over your ideal client. For example, if you are a pediatric nutritionist in private practice, a well-respected and well-liked pediatrician in your community may be a powerful influencer. Just one influencer could fill your practice or business. So the more influential your referral partners are, the more contact they have with your ideal clients, the fewer referral partners you will need.

Finding the decision makers

The "right people" to meet are the decision makers. When you network with those who ultimately influence the decision of who to hire, your efforts will pay off much more than networking with people who are less influential. While this may be true, do not assume that you know who the decision makers are and neglect to build relationships with others. James, a pharmaceutical salesperson, told me that many people assumed that they needed to get in front of the physicians and neglected to build relationships with others in the practice. However, when James built relationships with the administrative staff, including the office manager, he found himself in front of the physicians more readily. With the help of the support staff, he was able to build relationships with the decision makers. Because his relationships with the administrative staff were so pleasant, he enjoyed his meetings and presentations and didn't feel that he was pushing his way in or having to "sell" himself and his products.

Whatever you do, do not neglect relationships because you are trying to be efficient and get to the decision maker. Sales trainings often teach that you don't want to have a meeting unless the decision maker is present. I don't always agree with this philosophy. A friend told me a story of a horrible mistake along these lines: She and her husband were meeting with real estate agents to select one to sell their house. One agent they spoke with sounded knowledgeable over the phone, so she asked to set up a meeting with him. He asked when they could do it when her husband would be present. She said that her husband was traveling for work and so she was doing the meetings. He again tried to schedule it when her husband would be present. Clearly he was using the sales tactic of trying to meet only with the decision makers, assuming that she and her husband were equal or that he was more of the decision maker. She was turned off by this and did not schedule a meeting with him. Ironically, my friend (not her husband) was the decision maker about which real estate agent to select. Don't assume that you know who the decision maker is, and even if you do, do not neglect building other relationships.

Finding the Right People

ACTION STEPS

1. **Make a list of potential referral partners.** These are people who are already in contact with your ideal clients and who your ideal clients already know, like, and trust. Your list may be by profession, such as accountants, tax attorneys, and so on. If so, concentrate on one profession at a time so you can research potential referral partners and keep track of who you've contacted and the results. Don't spread yourself too thin or your follow-up (covered in Part 2) will suffer.

2. **Research networking opportunities.** If you aren't yet aware of ideal networking opportunities, research options. Ideally include some live events in your plans because connections that you make live in person are stronger than those that you make virtually over the phone or computer. Ask yourself the questions from the list above to determine which opportunities to pursue.

3. **Commit to attending events.** Once you've selected the best opportunities, put them on your calendar. Do not allow yourself to adopt

a "We'll see how things are going that day" approach, because there will inevitably be other things competing for your time, and you won't want to participate in the event.

4. **Connect with everyone, focusing on decision makers.** While we are trying to be focused, efficient, and strategic to save you time, you don't want to do these things at the expense of relationships that may prove valuable. Remember the golden rule and treat everyone as you'd want to be treated.

Filling a Need

Relationships are based on need fulfillment. Recent research by Dr. Sue Johnson, distinguished research professor at Alliant University in San Diego, California, and professor of clinical psychology at the University of Ottawa, Canada, has shown that couples that last fulfill one another's basic needs for attachment including closeness, security, and connection. Similarly, in business there are two parallel streams of needs that you need to fill.

1. **Emotional and intellectual needs.** People need to be able to like you, feel comfortable with you, and trust you. They need to feel that you are smart—not necessarily in an academic way, but in a very practical way. They need to feel that you know what you're doing.
2. **Bottom-line business needs.** Relationships that produce referrals and bottom-line results are most highly valued.

The only way to ascertain someone's needs is to ask questions and listen to the answers. Just as you don't want to assume who the decision maker is, you don't want to assume that you know what someone's true needs are.

Discovering the needs of your referral partner

My client Marjorie, a psychologist, told me that she frequently met with potential referral partners but nothing ever came of the meetings. In talking with her, I realized that she was mistakenly making the assumption that the people she met with were looking for more clients. She would talk about how she could refer to them and expect them to become engaged and interested, but in reality this rarely happened. Marjorie had done the difficult work of getting meetings with successful professionals. For the most part, these people had more clients and patients than they could handle. They did not want referrals. The idea of more clients stressed them out. When Marjorie learned to ask questions about their work and what their goals were, she found some fascinating things: Many people were looking to scale back their businesses. Others were looking to make a switch and work with different types of clients. Others didn't want to make any changes with their business but needed excellent referral sources for their clients. When Marjorie asked and listened to what people really needed, she was able to better connect with other professionals and help them meet their business goals.

Questions that you can ask to discover the needs of your referral partners include:

- In what direction are you heading with your business?
- What is your favorite type of client to work with?
- With what type of client do you work best?
- Is there anything that you're looking to change in your work?
- What are your current goals?
- What's the next chapter for your business?

If you find that someone doesn't have any needs in their business, then they are unlikely to be a potential referral partner.

Look for similarities and differences

Similarities are typically the foundation for personal relationships. People become friends over bonding about being a new mom, passion for a sports team, living on the same block, and so on. In professional relationships, things work differently. You need to have broad-based similarities but specific differences. Broad similarities include your philosophy or approach, background, or types of clients. There needs to be a fundamental match in values. For example, my closest business partners tend to be like me in the value we place on research-based approaches. For example, my colleague and friend, author of *The Psychology of Influence,* Kevin Hogan and I tend to be anti-guru ("This is what worked for me so it's what you should do") and pro-science ("This is what the research shows to work"). As such, I greatly enjoy collaborating with him—plus he is ridiculously smart and great at describing science in real-world language, something I am trying to learn. What important values guide your work? Who else shares such values?

Specific differences include factors such as the type of service or product you offer, your geographical location, and so on. Without these differences, there is no need for you because the other person does that same thing in the same way with the same people. One of my clients, Sarah, a business coach, told me that her best joint venture partners were also business coaches who were quite similar to her. The difference was the types of services that they offered. Sarah did intensive one-on-one work with clients while her business partners offered groups, workshops, and live trainings.

Start with your own needs

When looking for potential referral partners, people often think, "Who can refer to me?" Why not turn this process around and instead ask, "Who do I need to refer to?" Consider the types of professionals that your clients ask you for referrals for and the types of professionals that you recommend your clients meet with.

This approach is powerful because:

- **It is less intimidating and more enjoyable to approach someone from the perspective of how you can help them rather than how they can help you.** Because it tends to be nerve-wracking to initiate new business connections, it is important to consider what reduces the anxiety in the process. If you're coming from the place of needing a referral source or other resource for your clients, you are likely to feel more comfortable and less anxious.
- **It is genuine and authentic when you have a true need.** Building your professional database is one of the most important

things you can do. Put some thought into who you need to be in your list of contacts and why. Don't simply think of who you want to meet and then tell them that you'd like them to be in your database. This will feel and come across as lacking authenticity and sincerity.

- **You may not know their needs.** As we've discussed, we cannot always assume what another professional needs. When you begin from the place of what you need *for your clients*, you begin with what is known, and it serves as a great opening to then learn more about what the other person needs.

Let's say that you're a personal trainer building a large private practice. In thinking about who your clients may need, you come up with:

- Registered dieticians and nutritionists
- Weight loss coaches and consultants
- Sports medicine and rehabilitation physicians
- Physical therapists
- Massage therapists
- Acupuncture and acupressure specialists
- Image consultants, hairdressers, and others in the beauty industry

You can use this list of needs to fill in the skeleton of your professional database and then start finding the professionals to file under each category.

Consider who needs you

Keep close track of the source of your referrals. Record the type of person who referred you as well as the individual's name and contact information. For example, the personal trainer may have three categories of referral sources:

- Past clients
- Nutritionists
- Weight loss coaches

He would then look for trends. He may choose to add on to the professions who refer the most. Or he may choose to focus on adding new types of professionals who he does not yet have connections with. Either approach is valid. Collecting and analyzing the data of your referral sources enables you to come up with the strategy that works best for you.

Filling a Need

ACTION STEPS

1. **Know your business values.** Write down all of the things that you value in your professional life. These are the broad-based similarities that you will look to share with business associates. You may include things like "integrity, timeliness, sincerity," and so on.

2. **Know your differences.** Get clear on how exactly you and your services are different from others. This will help you to get out of a competitive mind-set and instead focus on your unique value.

3. **Build your referral database.** Use the format described above to build your list of professionals that your clients need.

4. **Practice discovering needs.** As you meet with people, practice asking the questions to discover what they really need. Once you know what drives them, you can best serve them. Look for psychological needs (calm, excitement, etc.), intellectual needs (professional growth and advancement, learning, etc.), and resource needs (time, money, etc.).

Initiating Conversations

This is the most challenging but also the simplest part of initiating relationships. We make it harder on ourselves than we need to. The bottom line is that you simply need to have a dialogue with someone to see if a synergy is there.

Going up to someone in person

This section will be very short. I am not a fan of contrived pickup lines and the like. Simply go up to someone and introduce yourself. "Hi, I'm Larina." You don't need anything fancy. If something else comes to mind—a compliment, an association, the way that you know the person, a mutual connection, or something else—that is great, but if not, that is fine too. Now, when you introduce yourself online or by voice mail, you will need to include more information, which you can glean from this next section.

Describing what you do

I love the dialogue that Michael Port describes in *Book Yourself Solid*. The key is that it is a meaningful back-and-forth dialogue. It starts, he says, with not giving your professional category as an answer to the question, "What do you do?" How can someone connect with a label like consultant, coach, doctor, speaker, real estate agent, and so on? Instead, identify what someone needs and how you fill it. Michael offers a formula:

- You begin: "You know how (insert the need of your audience)?"
- The other person responds.
- You say, "Well I (insert how you help people)…"

For example:

- **A financial planner.** "You know how people struggle with trying to decide how to invest their money? Well, I help them find the right mix of investments that fits their personalities and goals."
- **A real estate agent.** "You know how people have a vision of their dream home? Well, I help them find that home and get it for the best possible price."
- **A medical devices salesperson.** "You know how fast the fields of medicine and technology are changing? Well, I help hospitals stay on top of the best possible equipment based on the latest technologies."
- **A productivity coach.** "You know how common it is to rush through the day and end up feeling like you didn't actually get

anything done? Well, I help people prioritize their goals and get the most important ones on the calendar and checked off at the end of the day."

Don't feel that you have to have your opening committed to memory to be delivered verbatim. "Audio logos," elevator speeches, and other rehearsed openers often come across as too rehearsed. This undermines your authenticity and ability to connect with people. These openings also increase speaking anxiety because you get focused on yourself. The great thing about a dialogue like Michael Port's formula is that you have confidence that you have something to say that shows how you benefit others and engages people in a conversation. It becomes less about you and more about the needs of and benefits to others. This reduces your anxiety, increases your confidence, creates a connection, and enhances results.

Do speak with the passion, energy, and enthusiasm that accompanies your work and how you help clients. Get comfortable in describing what you do succinctly when someone asks you. It may not be the most comfortable thing to initiate conversations, but when you use the tools you'll learn here and get great results, you'll soon start to enjoy the process.

Rapport opens the door

In my doctoral training program, we took several classes on interviewing techniques. It was intimidating because you would need to interview someone while the entire class watched and the professor videotaped you. One day it was my turn to do the interview, and I was stressing out that I didn't remember any of the interviewing techniques I had learned. It suddenly occurred to me that I already knew what I needed to do in those first critical moments: establish rapport. Everything else was secondary.

Rapport is established largely through your nonverbal behaviors— your eye contact, relaxed posture, smiling, nodding, warm tone of voice, and mirroring of the other person's communication style so that you're in synchrony. You don't want to completely change your style, but you might modify it by 20 percent. If you're super high energy and loud and the other person is mellow and quiet, just tone your style down a bit. Where you sit can also make a difference. A 2011 *Psychology Today* article stated that women prefer sitting directly across from people, whereas men prefer to sit at an angle.

When you meet people, rather than getting overwhelmed by all of the things you hope to accomplish, keep your initial goal simple: establish rapport. The door will then be open for many more opportunities.

Initiating Conversations

ACTION STEPS

1. **Make it easy on yourself.** How have you been making this process harder on yourself than it needs to be? Are you trying to do too much or say too much? Are you trying to force things along more quickly than they naturally need to go? Experiment by stopping these things and see what happens.

2. **Get out of your head by using your senses.** Sometimes we get focused on how we'll introduce ourselves and what we'll say, and we don't listen to others. Avoid this by committing to being fully present. Listen to what others are saying. Smell the scents in the air. Feel the ground under your feet. These mindfulness skills will keep you out of your head and in the situation.

3. **Be aware of your nonverbals.** Establish rapport by maintaining an open, relaxed body posture, smiling, nodding, and mirroring the other person. Pay attention not to what is said but how you're saying it—your tone, pace, and volume of voice.

Now that you're ready to initiate relationships, let's explore one of the key ingredients in greater detail: how to attract attention.

Chapter 2

Grab Attention—
People Are Drawn to
These Five Things

Costumes and scenery alone will not attract audiences.

—*ANNA HELD*

EVERY DAY WE have millions of things competing for our attention. We don't have the time and mental energy to evaluate every person, e-mail, phone call, and opportunity that comes our way. Perhaps you can relate to this anecdote from one of my clients:

> *Last week I made dozens of phone calls and sent just as many e-mails. I need to expand my network and create new business opportunities, but I hate feeling like a pest, a telemarketer, or a spammer. I can't blame people for not getting back to me—I don't know if I would if I were in their position. We all have so much to do and are skeptical that someone wants something*

from us and will create even more for us to do. So, how can I get
attention and make a positive first impression so that people will
actually listen?

Getting your foot in the door can be the most challenging part of
building business relationships. The key is to instantly capture someone's
attention.

How Attention Works

Essentially, paying attention to something means that you concentrate on
one thing while you simultaneously don't concentrate on something else.
There are several types of attention, but we are most interested in "selective attention," which requires someone to tune out something else and
tune in to you. There are dozens of things with which you must compete
for attention, such as sites, sounds, physical sensations, thoughts, activities, and so on. If someone does not focus their attention on you, nothing
more can happen—people cannot hear your ideas, consider your value, or
remember you.

Our brains are designed to quickly shift attention. Imagine you are
walking along in the woods thinking about what's for dinner and you hear
a rustling sound. Your brain must quickly shift gears to check out that
sound—and be sure that what's for dinner is not you! Our goal is for you
to capture attention so that people are immediately interested in you, and
then sustain attention so that they want to learn more. We'll focus primarily on grabbing attention in this chapter because many of the topics we'll
cover later involve holding attention so you can further build relationships.

Researchers recently discovered that the brain processes something
that grabs attention (such as a rustling in the woods) differently than
something that requires sustained attention (such as mentally prepar-
ing your shopping list). In 2007, Massachusetts Institute of Technology
researchers Timothy J. Buschman and Earl K. Miller trained monkeys
to complete attention tasks on computers while their brain activity was
monitored. When monkeys were presented with something that grabbed
attention, such as a flashing object, the parietal cortex part of their brain
was engaged. The parietal cortex is a more primitive part of our lower

brains that keeps us focused on surviving. When, on the other hand, the monkeys were required to do something that required sustained attention, such as selecting something that looked different from other things, the prefrontal cortex region of their brains was engaged. The prefrontal cortex is the advanced part of our brains behind our foreheads that allows us to plan and strategize. So our first goal is for you to activate the parietal cortex and attract attention. Once you have successfully done this, the person's brain may be willing to engage the prefrontal cortex and start thinking about how you may work together.

Some of the things that we think should grab attention do not actually work. For example, in writing we may make something large and bold to grab attention; however, a good deal of research has shown that varying the size of something does not capture attention as powerfully as focusing on other variables does (and we'll cover these in this chapter). It can also be obnoxious to see gigantic headlines screaming out at you. Of course, you want your written headlines to stand out, so you can make them slightly larger or bold. What, then, is more important than size?

It turns out that there are five key things that grab attention and help people hear what you have to say.

Attention Grabber 1: Visual Imagery

Remember that our lower brains (parietal lobes) are involved with grabbing attention. This means that if you want to capture someone's attention, you actually don't want them to have to think a lot (which involves the more evolved frontal lobe). You've heard that a picture speaks a thousand words, and since you typically don't have a thousand words when you first come into contact with someone, visual images are crucial. In fact, your visual imagery will attract attention better than any words you use.

Between social media, e-mail marketing, viral videos, and other great technologies for connecting with people, you have many opportunities to grab attention. With most of these technologies, the visual component is primary in determining whether or not someone will be interested enough in you to respond to your e-mail, friend request, and so on.

A 2004 study of 1,363 print advertisement with 3,600 consumers investigated whether a business's brand, use of pictures, or text best captured attention. The researchers found that the pictorial element was the most effective at attracting the attention of consumers. This finding was true regardless of size, meaning that when comparing a small image versus large words, the small image was more powerful.

Yes, attractiveness is important

Superficial as it may be, we focus on that which we are attracted to. There is a psychology concept called "attentional adhesion," which means that attention can become fixed on something. A study by Florida State University researchers published as *Can't Take My Eyes off You* confirmed that our attention tends to become glued to people who we find attractive. Research conducted by Dustin Wood and Claudia Brumbaugh suggests that there tends to be a greater consensus among men than among women about what they view as physically attractive in the opposite sex. This research on attractiveness and attention does not mean that you need to be a supermodel to attract the attention of others. In fact, if you present yourself with too much sex appeal, people can become stuck on that and fail to consider business opportunities. If, for example, your image on your Web site is too attractive, people may not read your copy or take action. Since you have a *very* short amount of time to influence someone to take action, you do not want them to spend the narrow window of opportunity looking at your photo.

There are several things you can do, however, to enhance your attractiveness to others.

First, consider the headshot that you use in your marketing materials. In social media marketing, your image will make the first impression. Be sure that your photograph is in excellent focus, that the lighting is strong, and that the colors are vibrant. You can use neutrals if they are consistent with your brand, but even neutrals can be rich and clear in color. Definitely hire a professional photographer (it is less expensive than you may think), and be sure that you are comfortable with the person—if you are not, it will show in the photographs. If finances are an issue, hire a photography student from a local college. Bring at least three tops and two bottoms and (if applicable) do two to three hairstyles. For women, consider professional hair and makeup; it makes a big difference. If you want a more casual, approachable look, or if it goes along with your branding, take your photos outside. For example, one of my clients who owns a yoga studio recently had shots taken in various yoga poses outdoors on her yoga mat. Redo your headshot every couple of years, if you have a major change in your appearance, or if you change your target audience or business positioning. Be sure your headshot looks like you and reflects your personality—show it to friends and family for feedback.

Second, enhance physical appearance with contemporary and flattering hairstyles and clothing. Much of the gestalt or overall impression that we make is not based on our genetic features but on the way in which we present ourselves. Almost all of my clients have felt that they were right on track with their style and dress. When, however, I or an image consultant recommended changes, they experienced a positive impact on the impressions they made. They didn't see a problem before improvements were recommended. This is why it is important to get second and third opinions from professionals as well as from people whose style matches that of your ideal clients or referral partners. You want your overall look to

- **Make you feel confident.** Because this will impact your body language, a key component in ratings of attractiveness and positive first impressions.
- **Be consistent with your branding and style.** One of my clients, an executive coach, had a powerful, down-to-earth, tell-it-like-it-is style about his personality. When he'd go to meet with potential business connections, he wore a suit and appeared uncomfortable. In creating his branding, we adopted a more casual look that was consistent with his personality, communication style, and benefits to clients (he would tell it like it is and not sugarcoat things). As a result, he was more himself and he established closer and more rewarding business relationships.
- **Fit your audience.** This brings us to the next point . . .

Third, dress in the way that resonates with your audience. You need to wear what makes you feel most confident and comfortable, but do not neglect to consider your audience. In one study, 200 undergraduate students rated two measures of attraction: how much they would like a stranger and how much they would enjoy working with that person. The results indicated that the more similar students rated the strangers' style of dress to their own, the higher their ratings in both aspects of attraction.

Fourth, consider the attractiveness of anything that represents you. These are things such as your Web site, your office if you meet with prospects there, your handbag or briefcase, and so on.

Captivate with color

One of the most important aspects to consider in using imagery in your messaging is color. Color naturally evokes emotions (another one of the five attention grabbers). If you want people to feel stimulated and excited, choose colors like red or orange. If you want people to feel calm and relaxed, if you want to create an impression of trust and security, choose cool tones of blues and blue-greens. Yellow-greens evoke cheer and optimism.

Use attractive imagery in your marketing materials. Make sure that your business card, blog, Web site, and social media pages include colors and imagery that are likely to resonate with your target audience. Have a graphic designer create your Twitter background and other social media graphics using your great headshot (discussed above) and other imagery that will grab the attention of your prospective clients and referral partners.

For example, one of my clients runs wellness retreats for corporate women. The imagery she uses in her marketing includes a lot of nature scenes as well as shots of the women from previous retreats gathered together. The message these images convey is about relaxation, connection to nature, connection to others, and connection to oneself. She chose these types of things because these are the things her clients say they are hoping to get out of the retreat. When prospective clients see her marketing materials, they are immediately attracted to her services. They don't have to think about it. When her referral partners see her materials, they know that their clients would be attracted to her services, and they don't have to think about who to refer or how to refer them.

What type of imagery best fits you and your audience?

You can also utilize the other attention grabbers in your visual imagery to get a very powerful effect.

Attention Grabber 1: Visual Imagery

ACTION STEPS

1. **Get your new headshot taken.** Be sure to get a variety of poses, outfits, and backgrounds to use in different venues. Ideally, have a casual shot to use in social media and a more formal shot (if that is needed in your work) for your Web site. If your physique is important (for example, if you're a weight loss coach), be sure to get both your headshot and full body.

2. **Research color responses.** Conduct a mini-survey of those in your target market to see what colors people relate to the most. Include a few questions in which you give pictures that are similar with different colors. Maybe the first is you in three different color shirts, the next is three logos with different colors, the third is three photographs with different colors, and the fourth is four different color swatches. Ask people to pick their favorite for each. Do not ask them to explain their choices; you want their gut reactions.

3. **Gather feedback on your style.** Pay close attention to how your style fits your personal brand—is it warm and engaging? Down to earth? Professional and classic? Modern and cutting edge?

4. **Go to a nice department store and get fitted for a few new outfits.** Be sure to get them professionally tailored so they are as flattering as possible.

5. **Select two to three pieces of imagery to use throughout your marketing.** It may be your headshot plus your logo, your logo plus additional graphics, your headshot plus another photograph, and the like.

Attention Grabber 2: Unexpected Elements

The second aspect that immediately commands attention is contrast. The neuroscience term for this is salience, and it means how much something stands out in contrast to its surroundings. You would immediately notice a little green light flashing on your cell phone indicating a new message. Imagine that you are driving in the country and out the window you see cornfield after cornfield. Suddenly you notice a patch of sunflowers amid the corn. You cannot help but focus your attention on those bright sunflowers. The flashing light and the sunflowers are salient stimuli.

The reason that something unexpected stands out has to do with the scientific principle of habituation. Habituation means that we get used to something over time. For instance, if you enter a restaurant you may notice a strong smell. After you're in the restaurant for a couple of minutes, you don't notice it anymore; you've habituated to the smell. Habituation can happen with anything—smells, visual stimuli, emotions, sounds, temperature, and so on.

How can you use contrast to help yourself stand out? As we just discussed, visual elements are often the most important in attracting attention, so you can vary different aspects of visual design. One study by professors in Italy showed that varying color, form, and luminance (or brightness) is effective at capturing attention. For example, you may choose to use neutral colors in the background of your Web site or business card and bright colors in your logo or clothing to stand out. You can vary form by using contrasting fonts. You can manipulate luminance by using a strong light source in the headshot that you use in social media and making sure that the image is bright overall.

Also consider what naturally stands out about you and capitalize on those characteristics. If you tend to have a mellow, soothing voice and persona, when you go to frenzied networking meetings where people rush around trying to meet one another, emphasize the calm confidence in your voice and presence when you initiate conversations. If everyone goes up to each other with an opening line like, "So, what do you do?" begin conversations with something different, such as an observation, compliment, joke (but only if you're comfortable with humor—that one can backfire), or question.

Remember, however, that as we discussed in Chapter 1, we tend to like those who are similar to ourselves, so you want to be sure the contrast isn't so extreme that people feel you are too different and cannot relate with you. Using the example above, if someone is high energy and you are so mellow that they wonder if you have a pulse, that isn't good. Or if you attend a group where most people wear gray suits and white shirts, you don't necessarily need to wear a bright blue velvet suit, but you may wear a blue shirt with a navy suit. It doesn't take a lot to stand out and be recognized as different.

Attention Grabber 2: Unexpected Elements

ACTION STEPS

1. **Take the risk of standing out.** When you attend networking and other events to meet people, you'll be tempted to blend in. Don't. Tell yourself before you go that there's no point in wasting your valuable time going if you will not command attention. Wear a bright scarf or tie, introduce yourself in a unique way, or ask a thought-provoking question to stand out from the crowd.

2. **Incorporate contrast into your speaking engagements to gain and hold people's attention.** Consider varying your voice, gestures, distance from your audience, slides, and adding moments of silence.

3. **Use contrast in your visual marketing materials.** Draw attention to what you want people to notice by varying, color, form, or brightness.

4. **Use contrast in your voice mails.** Making sales calls is typically unsettling. As a result, we tend to either leave a fast generic message or a long rambling message. Instead, leave a short, punchy message using contrast by adding pauses, varying the speed of your voice, and so on. Your message will be more compelling and you will convey confidence.

Attention Grabber 3: Meaning

Have you ever been in a loud, crowded room and heard someone say your name? There are some things that we pay attention to no matter how busy we are. Your biggest challenge is to capture someone's attention while she is distracted with something else. Across research studies, two factors have emerged as consistently reliable ways to get attention, and a recent study showed that their power remains even when people's attention is engaged elsewhere:

- The person's name
- A smiley face icon

We cannot help but be attracted to the sound of our own name. We are also attracted to the names of people that we are close to, such as our children. Or names that we associate with, such as the name of our business. My favorite name in the world to hear is "Mommy." Refer to people by name as much as possible, but realize that if you do it too much, it will sound like you are using a sales tool on someone, and people do not like this. I think that the most natural times to use someone's name are at the beginning or ending of a conversation. For example, a pharmaceutical representative may say, "Hello, Dr. Stevens, how are you today?" and at the end, "Have a great day, Dr. Stevens!"

You can enhance your memory for pairing names with faces. You'll learn more about memory in Chapter 8, but for now practice combining someone's name with a key element about them. A colleague of mine has two daughters, Bella and Camilla. I remember that Bella is the older one because B is for bigger and B comes first in the alphabet. In the short term, you can remember someone's name by associating a feature, such as John in the blue shirt, but to remember something in the long term, you want to associate it with something meaningful. I would think, "John has bright blue eyes like my husband, John, has bright blue eyes."

E-mail marketers learned of the power of someone's name and began using names in subject lines of e-mails. I may receive an e-mail with the subject "Larina, what's the best way to grab attention?" While using names is powerful and certainly works, be wary of anything that everyone else is doing because then it violates Attention Grabber 2, and we habituate to it. This is similar to how parents use their child's name all the time, so when they really want to grab attention, they often add in the middle or last name as well: "Joey Allen, come here right now!"

If you don't know someone's name or you're addressing many people at once, another descriptor that applies to them is good (although not as good), such as the name of their city or something else that has meaning to them—the more specific the better. For example, singers often start their shows by saying the name of the city they're performing in: "Hello, Chicago!" When people hear something that they identify with—their name, the name of the organization, their company name, the name of their favorite sports team, and so on—their attention is captured and they begin to feel a connection to the speaker. Make it your goal to learn what people hold dear. These are the things that we can never tire of talking about. It may be their children, their neighborhood, environmental activism, their team, their car, their hundred-year-old house that they recently renovated, their pet. Learn what lights them up by asking open-ended questions and observing their reaction. If they are excited about something, their pupils may dilate and they may gesture more and become more animated. They'll speak more quickly and with more energy. Their posture will open up, and they'll smile more. They'll have stories and a lot to say.

Now let's turn to the second factor that grabs attention because of the meaning: a smiley face. It is interesting because we see smiley faces all the time, so why would they attract attention? It seems that our own name and a smiley face are more resistant to habituation than other things because of the meaning we associate with them. I would think and feel something different when a new contact says my name versus when my sister says my name. Additionally our brains are mentally primed to pay attention to these things. The meaning behind something also connects with Attention Grabber 5, emotion. When you have multiple attention grabbers in play, you achieve a compelling result.

While a smiley face icon is powerful, consider whether it fits with your brand image before beginning to use it. For many people, it will not be a good fit because it may be too cutesy or not in line with your professional image. I use smiley faces all the time because my brand is a bit casual and I like how they clarify things in writing. If you don't use smiley faces, consider what other words, symbols, or pictures would have special meaning for your audience and incorporate those. You can include a smiling face (in a photograph, for example) rather than the smiley face emoticon.

Attention Grabber 3: Meaning

ACTION STEPS

1. **Enhance your memory for people's names.** Practice learning people's names at every cocktail party, business function, or other event that you attend.

2. **Use people's names—in moderation.** Sales trainings often recommend using people's names, and then salespeople use their prospects' names at the beginning of every sentence, which violates the contrast rule and appears tacky. I recommend using someone's name once at the beginning and once at the end of a conversation.

3. **Practice remembering something unique about each person you meet.** Move on from conversations, but return to them later on and refer to the fact you've memorized about the person. For example, "Joe, I was thinking about your unique approach to estate planning and was interested in . . ."

4. **Brainstorm a list of what has meaning to your clients, referral partners, and other professional connections.**

5. **Refine your list of meaning by testing it out.** If you use social media, you can collect some great data by seeing what types of posts get the most comments or re-tweets.

6. **Include an emotional face.** Expressive faces get more attention, so smile in your headshot, use an image of an angry person (and follow up with a something like "How not to be this guy . . ." or "We know, dealing with lawyers can be infuriating—that's why we're different . . ."), or other emotional imagery.

Attention Grabber 4: Relevance and Clarity

You may have heard the expression in marketing, "What's in it for me?" The idea is that we listen to all new information with this question in

Attention Grabber 4: Relevance

ACTION STEPS

1. **Have a one-sentence message.** Practice saying what you do and how you help people out loud in one sentence or 30 seconds or less. Write it down and see if it is a run-on sentence that takes 10 lines or a crisp, succinct statement. Boil your message down so it is clear and concise.

2. **Do your homework.** Don't assume that you know what is relevant to someone. Learn. Read through their Web site. Sign up for their newsletter. Make it your mission to learn about what they care about and ask yourself if you fill a need.

3. **When you approach someone new, refer to something specific.** Please do not say, "I like your work and want to set up a call to discuss how we can work together." Instead, refer to something specific that you know about the person and a specific idea for collaboration.

4. **When presenting, immediately establish relevance.** Ask a powerful question, tell a quick compelling story. Show the audience how what you'll discuss matters to them.

5. **When presenting, emphasize your most relevant points.** No matter what you do, people will not pay attention to everything. It is hard to sort through a lot of material and figure out what to do with it. (That, incidentally, is why I include these action steps.) Highlight what is most important by using contrast features (varying tone, volume, visuals, etc.).

6. **Focus on only what is relevant at that moment.** Do not even get into everything that could be. If our attention capacities get overwhelmed, we shut down. Focus on one to three main ideas.

Attention Grabber 5: Emotion

Cognitive psychologists and neuroscientists often study attention that is controlled by the prefrontal cortex—the part of our brains behind our foreheads that is the most evolved part of the brain, responsible for attention, planning, and solving problems. There may also be a deeper part of our brain, emotional parts (such as the limbic components in cingulate cortex and amygdala), involved. We attend to and remember emotion. In one study, three patients who had strokes (in the right parietal part of their brain) showed a greater ability to remember faces with strong emotional expressions, including happy or angry, than faces with neutral expressions.

There are two ways to use emotion:

- Convey your own emotion.
- Stimulate an emotional reaction in someone else.

How can you convey your own emotion? One way is in your headshot. If you're trying to decide between a headshot with a professional, neutral look and one with a happy expression, go for the happy one if you want to be remembered. People judge expressions of happiness in part by how much our eyes squint or crinkle at the corners. Crow's feet can make you look happier, so go easy on the Botox and model-type smiles where your eyes are wide open and you have a painted on smile.

Another way is in your expressiveness. Allow your nonverbal communication to convey how you feel—whether it is serious, passionate, relaxed, or cheerful—with your tone of voice (the feeling in your voice), pitch (how high or low it is), speed (how fast or slow), and volume (how soft or loud), and your body language (how you move, your gestures, posture, and facial expression). Know that if your verbal communication (what you say) and nonverbal communication (how you say it) do not match, people trust your nonverbal communication. Performers sometimes use contrast in verbal and nonverbal communication to keep their audiences focused and engaged, such as telling a hilarious joke with a poker face. I don't recommend this unless you're a stand-up comic, but you can see how effectively emotion (or the absence of emotion) can be used to focus attention.

We often try so hard to be "professional" that we neglect to show our emotions and attract attention. If you're so emotionally controlled that you come across as professional but no one pays attention or is attracted to you and what you have to offer, you have not accomplished anything. Let your personality show; you'll feel more authentic and establish better bonds with people.

How can you stimulate an emotional reaction in someone else? You'll get a lot of ideas for this in the next chapter.

Attention Grabber 5: Emotion

ACTION STEPS

1. **Be expressive.** Convey emotion. Don't sacrifice the ability to attract and capture attention to be overly "professional."

2. **Know that emotion can be subtle.** You don't have to go over the top, but don't overly censor yourself either. Remember that emotion is conveyed not just in your facial expression but also in your body language, movement, eye contact, and so on.

3. **Select an emotional headshot.** Even if it is not your most attractive image, select one that sends a feeling and connects with people.

4. **Combine contrast with emotion.** If you smile the entire time you talk with someone, your smile will lose its salience. Instead have an open facial expression and smile for emphasis.

Now that I have your attention, let's move on to one of the most important things you can do in your marketing: engage emotion.

Chapter 3

Engage Emotion—
People Respond to Feelings,
Stories, and Metaphors

If you have zest and enthusiasm you attract zest and enthusiasm.
Life does give back in kind.

—NORMAN VINCENT PEALE

THINK ABOUT SOMEONE who you recently met. Did you get a vibe about them and walk away thinking, "I liked her," or, "I didn't really like her"? Essentially we like people who make us feel good and don't like people who don't make us feel good.

Your most important goal is to create positive feelings in the other person. Being liked is one of the essential, if not the most essential, components of business success. Research has shown that likeability strongly influences personal and professional success. Likeability also influences the success of advertisements. In a study of advertisements on Dutch television over the course of a decade, researchers found that commercials that viewers rated as less likeable produced less effective results.

Clearly you want to be likeable, and you want your marketing to be likeable. So how do you do that? The most powerful way is to evoke positive emotions in others.

Evoke Positive Emotions

One reason that being likeable and arousing a positive mood is so important is that people tend to be skeptical of a message when they first hear it. Dr. William McGuire of Yale University has extensively researched what makes people believe or disbelieve a message. He found that the most important consideration is the source of the message: you. If someone knows, likes, and trusts you, she will be less skeptical of your message. Another important variable is the mood that the person receiving your message is in. You can impact that too because emotions are contagious.

Emotion is contagious

In *Primal Leadership,* emotional intelligence researchers Daniel Goleman, Richard E. Boyatzis, and Annie McKee explain how the mood of leaders is contagious. We have mirror neurons in our brains that cause us to take on the emotions of others, especially leaders. This concept of emotional contagion is one reason why emotional intelligence is so important—you can directly influence how people feel with your mood. And when people feel good, they are more prone to like you and want to do business with you. You can learn more about emotional intelligence and read an interview with Dr. Annie McKee in my book *The Confident Leader.*

Be sure that you're in a positive mood as you make your business connections. If you aren't having a great day, take a few minutes to do something to boost your mood before an important networking event or meeting. Your mood booster may be listening to a favorite song, sitting outside in the sun and enjoying a cup of coffee, or going on a quick walk. You'll feel better and so will the person with whom you meet.

Emotion is immediate

The vibe or emotional response we get from someone is immediate. We can usually tell in a matter of seconds if we feel we have "chemistry" with someone. This may be why speed dating programs such as 8minuteDating are so popular. I think it could actually be even speedier—eight seconds. We tend to know that quickly if there is a connection. It is similar in business. While you aren't looking for a dating relationship, you are typically looking for someone you like. For the most part, we tend to do business with those we like, which is a combination of how we feel about them as a person and the benefit that they can bring to our business.

In the first few seconds of meeting someone, your goal is twofold:

1. Be warm, engaging, and likeable so people see your personality and get a good vibe.
2. Engage curiosity so people want to learn more.

The tools I shared in Chapter 2 on capturing attention serve to stimulate one of the most important emotions in building connections: curiosity.

Emotion results from specific behaviors

There are three ways to impact emotion in yourself and others: thoughts, biology, and behaviors. Typically, the easiest thing to influence is your behaviors. Let's review *what not to do*. Here is a list of the top 10 most common mistakes I've seen my clients make. Note that the way I determined these is from watching people live at events or listening to them over the phone on conference calls. They are not things that people tell me that they do—most of us are unaware of these types of things.

1. Not Being Friendly What does it really mean to be friendly? It isn't so much about how you act as how you make the other person feel. Being friendly involves communicating your openness and interest in another person. It entails expressing warmth, interest, and comfort. When I observed clients make this mistake, it was not typically because they were unfriendly people, although a few needed to work on expressing their friendliness more outwardly. More commonly, a lack of friendliness seemed to be because they were too focused on delivering a pitch or elevator speech and were therefore less focused on connecting with the other person.

2. Being Overly Professional This mistake is related to friendliness. Because you are a smart, educated professional, you may feel that it is most important to lead with that to establish your expertise. As we will discuss in the next chapter, showing expertise is critical but not at the expense of showing friendliness, openness, and warmth.

3. Not Expressing Interest and Curiosity This manifests behaviorally through asking questions. When you ask thoughtful, specific questions in a way that expresses genuine interest and curiosity, you will be perceived as more likeable. In addition, you will learn more about the person, which will help with everything else we're discussing. While it is crucial that you're prepared to meet with people, sometimes you can be too prepared. You assume that you know what they want and launch into a sales pitch when really your initial goal at this stage in a relationship is to be curious and find out exactly *what they see* their needs as being.

4. Being Calculating or Overtly Self-Serving You know that feeling when you talk with someone and you can almost see the wheels turning in his mind as he tries to figure out how you can help him? That is not good. Of course our goal is to create relationships that get results, but you don't need to think so specifically about how someone could help you at this stage in the game. If you find yourself doing this, become more present in the moment by observing, listening, and asking questions.

5. Not Being Genuine As excited as you may be to meet someone and about the prospect of doing business with them, be careful to stay true to your most important values. It can be tempting to start agreeing with everything or to say that you do things that are not your true area of expertise. This can create a very slippery slope and can come across as lacking sincerity and simply telling people what they want to hear.

6. *Trying Too Hard* The way to recognize if you're trying too hard is to ask yourself two important questions:

- What am I afraid will happen?
- What am I doing to prevent that from happening?

When a relationship or opportunity is important to us, we often experience anxiety about messing it up. In turn, we tend to overcompensate and try too hard. This behavior can mask your true personality, undermine the perception of your value, and prohibit a connection between you and the other person.

7. *Being Too Generic* Don't be afraid to put your stake in the sand and show exactly what you stand for and what you do and don't do. It always amazes me how often people state what they do in a generic way that we've heard a hundred times before. For example, I role-played with a client about how she presented herself in networking situations. When I asked her what she does she said, "I'm a life coach. I help people unlock their true potential." Her response was too general and didn't show her unique value and personality.

8. *Not Focusing and Listening* Nothing feels worse than talking with someone as they look over your shoulder, scanning the room for their next encounter. If someone makes us feel uninteresting or unimportant, we immediately do not like them. If you are going to take the time to speak with someone, make it quality time. In just a couple of minutes, you can forge an important connection that you can follow up on later if you need to speak with more people at that time. If you can't commit to focusing on a conversation, do not allow yourself to have it.

9. *Being Guarded* People sometimes seem to want to appear mysterious in order to arouse curiosity. While curiosity is important, being guarded, evasive, or mysterious is annoying. Don't make people do a lot of work to get to know you. They either won't do it or they'll leave frustrated and energy depleted.

10. ***Pretending to Understand*** Let's say that you're speaking with someone who has a lot of technical expertise that you do not understand. Decide whether it is something that you want and need to understand or not. If so, ask the questions to learn more. If not, say so in a way that compliments the other person's knowledge and is upfront about the limits of your understanding. Do not, however, say yes and pretend that you understand because you don't want to appear dumb. Doing so digs a huge hole for yourself and limits your realness.

Your awareness of these specific behaviors that foster or hinder likeability and emotional connection will help you and the other person feel confident and at ease.

Evoke Positive Emotions

ACTION STEPS

1. **Be self-aware.** Self-awareness is the foundation of emotional intelligence, and emotional intelligence is the foundation for likeability and business success. Observe your thoughts, feelings, and behaviors as an outside observer would, without being attached to them or defensive. Know your patterns of responding in different interpersonal situations.

2. **Be a mirror.** Because you will influence others with your emotions, reflect the emotions you hope they will have. If you want people to feel calm and relaxed in your presence, speak a bit more slowly and softly. If you want people to feel cheerful, be upbeat and energetic. If you are not feeling this way at the moment, influence your own emotions through self-talk, music, exercise, or a conversation with a colleague, friend, or family member.

3. **Be more of yourself.** This hardly sounds like an action step, but it is. Be sure that you aren't being influenced by your own fears and insecurities and overcompensating. Own your personality and strengths, and don't try to be something you're not. For example, if you're more introverted, naturally you don't need to try to be a stand-up comic. Instead, capitalize on your strength of connecting with people deeply one on one.

4. **Videotape and audiotape yourself.** It's hard to know how we really come across if we don't take a step back and watch or listen. It may be challenging to videotape yourself in a real-world setting, so you may need to do this with a coach. You can easily audiotape yourself during phone conversations or teleseminars (with the other person's consent, of course). You can make a list of a few important dimensions such as warmth, friendliness, and interest and rate yourself on a scale of 0–5 for each. If you can get additional ratings from others as well, that is ideal. Pay particularly close attention to your nonverbal behaviors (tone of voice, posture, facial expression) because they more strongly communicate a message than what you say.

5. **Have a friend nearby.** You're more likely to be relaxed and be yourself if someone you know is around. Work your way up to attending events by yourself once you have gained comfort and developed your friendly professional persona.

6. **Ask specific, thoughtful questions.** Listen closely to what the other person is saying and ask yourself, "What interests me?" or "What do I truly not understand or want to learn more about?" Asking yourself questions like these leads to genuine questions and displays of interest. If you need a second to think of such a question, take it, rather than saying something just to say it.

The Sound of Your Brand

Emotion can be influenced in interesting ways. For example, did you know that the name of your company can influence emotion—and not just because of the connotation of the word? For example, a name like Kim's Cookies can make us happy because we love cookies. But there's another reason: recent research has shown that the sound of a brand can create positive emotions. In particular, a name that includes repetition of sound was found to generate positive feelings in those who heard the name. Kim's Cookies is pleasing because of the repetition of the *k* sound. This attraction to repetitive sounds may be hardwired. I remember when my son began talking, he would get so excited saying sounds that repeated:

"Mommy, mommy, mommy!" Repeated sounds are easy on the ears and make us feel good.

On the flip side, complicated sounds or names that people cannot pronounce lead to negative emotions. You might not want to change your name, but you can use a difficult to pronounce name to your advantage. You can call yourself Nancy "G" or Dr. "B." This not only reduces the negative emotions people would experience if they couldn't say your name, but it sounds familiar and friendly, which enhances likeability. Assuming that others in your field are not doing it, it also uses the Attention Grabber 2 and helps you stand out. You could also give a mnemonic. People are not always sure how my name is pronounced, so I sometimes say, "Larina like a boat marina." Just be sure that what you are associating yourself with has a pleasant meaning.

Sounds and Simplicity

ACTION STEPS

1. **Revisit the sound of your brand.** Say it out loud. Ask other people to say it out loud. If possible, revise it to add phonetic repetition or simplify the sound. Be sure that it is easily pronounceable.

2. **Consider a separate brand.** If you're debating whether to brand based on your name or to create a separate business brand, consider how your name sounds. If it sounds like something you don't want to be associated with or is difficult to pronounce, consider a separate brand.

3. **Name programs to make people feel good.** If you offer your services in programs (which is a good idea), say the names of the programs out loud. Do the sounds of the programs make people feel happy? If a personal trainer had a program called "Lose Weight at Any Age," she could rename it "Fit at 40 in just 4 weeks" to include phonetic repetition.

Tell Stories to Engage Emotion

Throughout history, stories have been one of the most powerful ways that people communicate ideas and share emotions. You can use stories to engage people's emotions in

- One-on-one conversations
- Group conversations
- Presentations
- Audio and written materials on your Web site or social media profile
- Pitches and proposals

How to tell stories that engage emotion

You may remember that I've mentioned how in communications, the "how" is more important than the "what." This means that how you say it is more important than what you say.

When you've done a quick read of the situation or planned a story as part of a presentation, you'll have a good sense of how much time you have. Own that time and use it to make the story engaging and add a little drama. Pause briefly before key points. Speak with more energy and more quickly when you get to exciting points. Ask questions. These may be questions that you want someone to answer in a dialogue or something that you want them to think about. For example, "Can you imagine what she did at that point?"

In terms of what you say, think of your story like a picture book for a young child. There are three key components:

- A beginning, a middle, and an end.
- Great illustrations. Our emotional brains process imagery more readily than language. The goal of your story should be to paint a picture.
- Simplicity and one clear moral of the story.

In addition to the visual sense, you may draw other senses into your stories as well. Sensory perception and emotion go hand in hand. Have you ever walked into a room with the smell of freshly baked apple pie or cookies and felt comfortable and happy? Certain scents, such as vanilla and lavender, are associated with pleasurable feelings. Even thinking about these scents (without actually smelling them) can stimulate the brain to produce the positive emotion. So including the five senses (sight, smell, touch, sound, and taste) in your stories makes the stories not only more interesting, but more emotionally powerful.

The bottom-line storytelling technique

People sometimes hesitate to tell stories because they are afraid that they will take too long. You can tell a full story or give a brief version. If you have only a limited window of time, a good way to give a brief version of the story is to share the outcome or bottom line. For example, a financial advisor might say to a real estate agent, "I recently worked with this great young professional couple and helped them figure out how to save for their down payment on their dream home, so they may be in need of your services soon." The real estate agent then has the opportunity to ask questions about the story of how the couple created their savings plan or about how they may be in need of her services. Either way, the story grabs attention, piques curiosity and interest, and creates a desire to learn more.

Have a background story

I love it when I hear the name of a company or a program and there's a story that goes behind it. When my clients are working on branding their businesses, I suggest that they list names associated with important stories from their personal or professional lives. This is a great way to bring ideas to life and infuse them with emotion. One of my clients, a bright, creative leadership consultant named Zita, thought of a story about how one of her three sons once refused to eat his breakfast. He said that he'd rather put jam on a stone from the garden and eat that. Zita then went out and got a stone, put some apricot jam on it, and playfully served it to him on a nice plate (I told you she is bright and creative). She named her business PebbleJam, and the story serves as a metaphor for how leaders develop with her services. It also creates a wonderful visual, which you now know is key to attracting attention and engaging emotion.

The other background story that you want to have is your own story. How and why you got into the work that we're doing. This story shows the reason that you're passionate about what you do. As the quote in the beginning of the chapter shows, zest and enthusiasm attract zest and enthusiasm. Another important benefit of your story is that it provides listeners with a sense of coherence about you—what you do and who you are fit together. It just feels right. This sense of coherence is calming and relaxing. It also establishes trust and credibility, which we'll discuss in the next chapter.

Tell Stories to Engage Emotion

ACTION STEPS

1. **Come up with a handful of stories.** Have your best stories ready to go by thinking of which stories people tend to respond well to and which stories best illustrate what you do, how you help people, why someone would be interested in working with you, and so on. Commit these stories to memory by writing them out in the following format:

   Beginning:

   Middle:

   End:

   Don't memorize the story verbatim, but know what falls under each component. Write two versions of your stories, short and long, and then get practice telling them as much as possible.

2. **Test out your stories.** As you prepare a story for a presentation, ask a few people to listen to you tell it and then have them fill out a brief questionnaire about the feelings evoked. For example, your questions may be:

Rate how much the story made you feel the following emotions on a scale of 0 (not at all) to 5 (very much):

Happy

Hopeful

Inspired

Curious

Optimistic

3. **Practice the bottom-line story.** If you do interviews on television or radio, you have a very brief period of time to answer questions, such as 30 seconds. Practice telling a bottom-line story in less than one minute. Whether or not you do media interviews, this skill will come in handy.

Use Metaphors to Engage Emotion

One of the most powerful ways to reach people on a deep level is through metaphors. In marketing ourselves and our services, our ultimate goal is for someone to hear something and think, "Wow, I *need* that." Or "Wow, my clients *need* that." This sense of needing something is typically unconscious. We simply experience an emotional reaction to something but are not sure why.

In the book *Marketing Metaphoria*, Harvard Business School professor Gerald Zaltman and coauthor Lindsay Zaltman discuss the power of deep metaphors. They explain that deep metaphors and emotions are closely linked because both are universally experienced on an unconscious level and seem to be a combination of being hardwired in our brains and stemming from our experiences. In their research, which consisted of conducting 12,000 interviews of consumers of products and services in more than 30 countries, seven fundamental deep metaphors accounted for 70 percent of all deep metaphors:

1. **Balance.** This may include physical balance (such as being on or off center), psychological balance (such as feeling on or off track), and social or moral balance (feeling that something is fair or unfair). Positive emotions associated with feeling balanced may include feeling at peace, calm, serene, satisfied, and comfortable.

2. **Transformation.** This has to do with something changing to something else. It may be something that happens in nature, such as a tadpole turning into a frog, or with a phase in life, such as going from being an employee to being a business owner. Someone who shows a transformation metaphor may value excitement, adventure, newness, creativity, and change.

3. **Journey.** This is the process of moving from something to something else. It may be fast or slow, short or long, easy or hard, rewarding or grueling, and so on. Feelings and values involved in a journey metaphor may include curiosity, interest, intrigue, or leadership.

4. **Container.** This is the sense of keeping something inside (or keeping something out). A container may be associated with a positive emotion, such as feeling cozy and secure, or a negative emotion, such as feeling trapped.

5. **Connection.** This is our sense of relatedness and belonging with others. Connection may be desirable or undesirable when someone does not want to be associated with something or someone. Positive emotions associated with the connection metaphor include a sense of fitting in, support, understanding, relationship, unity, and bond with others.

6. **Resource.** This is the most fundamental of deep metaphors because it is linked with our survival. Feeling as though we lack resources is likely to be linked with fear and panic, while feeling as though we have resources is likely to be linked with comfort (although not necessarily contentment).

7. **Control.** This is related to the feeling that you are in charge of your life. Some people have a higher need for control while others may be more flexible. Feeling out of control is often associated with anxiety, whereas feeling in control is often associated with feeling organized, powerful, influential, and disciplined.

How do you know which deep metaphors are important?

Determining which metaphors to evoke and what language to use entails listening. Take note of the way in which people speak, the imagery that is evoked, and what patterns you notice.

Let's say, for example, that you're a financial planner and you notice that your prospective client has said, "I am the breadwinner," "Cash burns a hole in my pocket," and "I need to pay for my son's college." This individual appears to view money and therefore financial planning as a resource. Understanding this metaphor enables you to speak about how you help your clients manage the resource of money. Knowing that a lack of resources is associated with fear and panic, you can choose to discuss how you work with clients to select secure investments. Let's say that another financial planning prospect says, "Saving has been an uphill battle," "It is tough when the stock market is down," and "I'm moving up the corporate ladder." Observing this type of language enables you to see that this person sees their financial planning needs as a journey. As such, you may evoke the image of savings accumulating like a mountain, or how you help clients take the burden of not knowing what to do off of them so they no longer feel like they're pushing a boulder up a mountain.

The other way to determine what metaphors resonate with your prospective clients or referral partners is to test them out. Select the top few metaphors that you believe are most relevant and use language associated with each. Observe people's responses.

One of my clients, Jarrod, a career coach who helped executives in transition, did this with his clients. Based on his experience, he predicted that the metaphors most relevant to his clients were transformation, journey, connection, and control. He used language such as "career transition" and "career change" to capture the transformation metaphor. For journey, he spoke of "the long trip," "crossing into new fields," and "as you travel through your career." For connection, he said things like "the right fit," "the relationship between your skills and job," and "hitting it off with colleagues." For control, he said things like "be in charge of your career" and "get back in the driver's seat." He found that his clients responded most favorably to the journey and relationship metaphors. Even more interestingly, he was able to see how male and female clients, clients of different ages, and clients in different fields responded differently. He used this knowledge to shape his marketing materials, including the language and imagery he selected. He also used it to determine the stories he would tell, and he selected different stories to share based on who he was speaking with and in what setting.

Use Metaphors to Engage Emotion

ACTION STEPS

1. **Look over your notes.** Go over your notes from your initial meetings with prospective clients and referral partners and see if you notice any themes or metaphors arise in how they describe their needs.

2. **Take notes verbatim.** Begin collecting data about the metaphors that most resonate with your clients by writing down exactly what they say in quotes. Listening for metaphors is like reading between the lines; it requires practice. You may have difficulty doing it on the spot, so take good notes and review them after your first meeting. Make the goal of your first meeting to be friendly, connect and engage positive emotions as we discussed earlier, and practice the metaphor piece afterward.

3. **Test out various imagery.** Imagery is the most powerful way to connect with metaphors. Present current clients or referral partners with a few images and ask them which they like best. They don't need to explain why. For example, the owner of an advertising firm may have an image of a design team meeting with a client (connection, showing that the client values collaborating on the process) or a gift wrapped up (container, showing how the client would like to receive their advertising campaign).

4. **Know your own metaphors.** Think about what you value personally and professionally and what metaphors most influence you. It is fine to select a couple or even a few metaphors. The more you understand this process, by doing it with yourself, the more you will be able to do it with others. You may also choose to do your branding around the metaphor that means the most to you, knowing that you'll attract people with similar values.

Now that you've attracted attention and engaged emotion, you want to show how you're the go-to person, the credible expert in your field. Let's go there now.

Chapter 4

Establish Credibility— People Want to Work with Trustworthy Experts

---

In the end, you make your reputation and you have your success based upon credibility and being able to provide people who are really hungry for information what they want.

—*BRIT HUME*

YOU SHOULD SEE my father's basement. He's an antiques dealer and appraiser. This means that my parents' house is basically a museum housing his antiques collection. His basement is filled to the brim with incredible artwork—everything from Mexican wedding vases to brightly colored quilts to this strange square piece of wood with half of a bowling ball on top and a dozen metal holes of various sizes. Can you guess what that is? It's a device to measure your thumb size for a bowling ball. How would he have ever known that there was some value in a piece like that? Over the years, he educated himself and has become an expert on art and antiques.

He has found highly valuable paintings and sculptures at household sales that later sold at major auction houses all over the world.

I once asked my dad, "When you're sorting through a ton of stuff at garage sales and antiques shops, how quickly can you tell if you're interested in pursuing something?"

"Instantly," he said.

"You mean in a matter of minutes?"

"No, less than that. Seconds. Probably less than a second."

"And then what do you do?" I asked.

"It depends if I have time. Often I have to make an immediate decision. If I have the time, I focus on the sensible things to look into—quality, artist, signature, and so on."

Similarly, his clients make immediate decisions about whether or not he has credibility as an art and antiques appraiser and dealer to be entrusted with their valuable collections. We all do this. Every day we're forced to make immediate decisions about whether or not something is credible, relevant, or valuable to us. Credibility is the basis for all relationships—without it, people will not take the time to listen to us, trust our message, or want to do business with us.

What Determines Credibility?

Do you know whether you're perceived as credible? Let's look into the factors that make up credibility.

The four types

In the early 1950s, Yale University researchers Carl Hovland, Irving Janis, and Harold Kelley created a model to explain what makes a message be perceived as credible. They found that credibility resulted from a perception of the communicator's trustworthiness and expertise.

More recently, researcher B.J. Fogg expanded the model to include four key types:

1. **Presumed.** This type of credibility is based on ideas and assumptions people hold.

the back of our minds. The Attention Grabber principle behind this is relevance. You may use the other attention grabbers and get someone to notice you for a split second, but if your information is not relevant to them, you will not actually grab their attention long enough for anything to happen.

Remember that our initial goal is to make people *not* have to think. When you lack a clear message, people may be interested in you (often because of one of the other attention grabbers), but your message is too diffuse to grab their attention. It requires too much work for them to try to figure out exactly what you do and how you can help them or their clients.

In order to immediately show your relevance, you may need to do some background investigation. Relevance relates closely with the last principle about meaning—if you can show how you and your ideas are personally meaningful to someone, you will be relevant and command their attention. I recently gave a keynote address to an association of interior designers. Before my talk, I conducted a brief three-question survey of the members of the organization. I began the talk: "What are the three most common problems in marketing an interior design business? Here's what *you* told me . . ." My information was immediately relevant to them.

Before contacting or meeting with someone new, be sure that you have done your homework and can quickly show how what you do is relevant to them. To be relevant, you must show your key similarities and how you fill a need, as we discussed in Chapter 1.

Sacrifice what is not relevant. We often want to throw everything out there in hopes that something will stick. This is like those English class essays we wrote in high school where we included everything but the kitchen sink, hoping to get those +1 points in red ink for everything that counted. Don't do this. The only way relevance works is when it is very simple. Do not even bring up things that are not immediately relevant. You might make a note to yourself to discuss certain opportunities in the future, but remember that when it comes to relationship building, the key is to go *one step at a time*. If you were on a first date and you started talking about how many kids you wanted to have and what you wanted to name them, you might not get a second date.

2. **Reputed.** This is based on other people's experiences and can be seen through testimonials, referrals, and endorsements.
3. **Surface.** This is based on initial observation and first impressions and tends to be visual in nature.
4. **Earned.** This is based on our own experiences with something or someone and develops over time.

In 2007, Maria Mattus of Linköping University, Sweden, set out to determine how Fogg's four types of credibility came into play as students evaluated the credibility of scientific information on the Web. The four elements that students rated as most important actually fell into each of Fogg's four categories: whether the author of the paper was an established researcher (presumed credibility), teachers' recommendations (reputed credibility), the year of publication (surface credibility), and their experience of the abstract (earned credibility). Thus, it appears that all four of these types of credibility come into play as students evaluate information online, and are likely to come into play as people evaluate us online.

Credibility on the Web

When you meet a new business contact, one of the first things she will do is look you up online. Most likely the first site she will find is your Web site. How long does it take for people to form an impression of your Web site? According to research by Gitte Lindgaard and her colleagues at Carleton University in Canada, the length of time is almost impossible to conceive—50 milliseconds. This is equal to about one-twentieth of a second. Most people do not have any conscious thought process during this length of time.

Do you know what people would think if your Web site flashed by them for one-twentieth of a second? Our goal of course is to make them think—or, more accurately, feel—something positive. You also want to feel something positive about your site. I recently had my sites and social media graphics redesigned by One Lily Creative Agency, and now I love the way they look and I feel proud to share them.

Stanford University's Persuasive Technology Lab, in collaboration with Sliced Bread Design LLC and Consumer Reports WebWatch, set out to discover what aspects of Web sites people deem as credible or not.

This study was the first to determine what people notice about Web sites and how those things impact their feelings about the site.

A creative recruitment method, where nonprofit groups let their supporters know that their participation in this study would result in a $5 donation, resulted in 2,684 people participating. Participants were randomly assigned to one of 10 content categories: e-commerce, entertainment, finance, health, news, nonprofit, opinion, search engine, sports, or travel. They were then given two Web sites in their category and asked to rank them and provide comments. The results yielded 2,440 comments that were sorted into different categories.

The Most Important Measures of Credibility

- **46.1 percent: Design look.** This is related to the overall professionalism and look and feel of the site.
- **28.5 percent: Information design and structure.** How organized and easy to navigate the site is.
- **25.1 percent: Information focus.** Some respondents showed preference for simple and narrowly focused information while others appreciated breadth of information provided.
- **15.5 percent: Company motive.** Sites that seemed to have selling something as the only motive lost credibility in ratings.
- **14.8 percent: Information usefulness.** This category was most important for health and entertainment sites and least important for sports and nonprofit sites.
- **14.3 percent: Information accuracy.** People assessed whether the information was consistent with what they knew from previous readings and television reports.
- **14.1 percent: Name recognition and reputation.** Greater familiarity led to a greater sense of perceived credibility.

As you can see from the data, the look of the site was the most important factor, which was prioritized a bit more often with the sites in finance (54.6 percent), search engines (52.6 percent), and travel (50.5 percent) versus news (39.6 percent) and nonprofit (39.4 percent) sites. Many of us like to think that design is not that important so we don't have to hire a professional design firm, but it turns out to be the most important factor in determining whether or not your site and you are perceived as credible.

What Determines Credibility?

ACTION STEPS

1. **Find out how the site makes people feel.** To be sure your site has the look and feel you want, survey people in your target audience and ask them to rate the site from 0 to 5 on five key dimensions: professionalism, overall feel, how much they like it, how clean and clear it is, and how (fill in the blank with an adjective you want people to feel: relaxed, energized, happy, curious, hopeful, etc.) it makes them feel.

2. **Make sure your navigation is organized**. Think about this from the user's perspective. Do they know the difference between options like services, products, and programs? Probably not, so pick just one.

3. **Be sure the design scheme is clean and cohesive.** Often our sites evolve over time, and things begin to get tacked on as our business changes. If this is the case, it is time for your site to be redesigned. Think of a site like a computer—it's unlikely that the same one will continue to work for you for five years. Most of the strategies you're learning in this book are free or very low-cost. Your Web site is a good place to invest a decent percentage of your marketing budget.

4. **If your primary site is a blog, the same rules apply.** The one exception is that blogs can be easier to maintain if you are just adding content and not reworking the design. At the minimum, hire someone to help you set up your blog and have a graphic designer create your banner. The most cohesive looks result when a Web design firm designs the site in WordPress or whatever blog platform you use (rather than uploading a banner and doing the rest yourself).

5. **Organize content clearly and avoid advertisements.** Make use of headings and categories so people know what to find where. Consider how people look for information. Depending on the time sensitivity of your topic, it may not matter if you wrote something in July 2010. Rather, they may prefer a heading like "How to Write a Business Plan in One Day." Unless the primary purpose of your site is to make money from ads,

avoid advertisements since they reduce credibility. Be most concerned with the "above the fold" part of the site. This is the part that people see before they need to scroll down.

6. **Read *Trust Agents: Using the Web to Build Influence, Improve Reputation, and Earn Trust* by Chris Brogan and Julien Smith.** It is an excellent resource for learning how to build trust online in new media. Follow @chrisbrogan on Twitter to see how he does this himself. He has a wonderful way of connecting with his 184,000 (as of July 2011) followers.

Know Your Audience

As with any form of communication, credibility is in the eye of the beholder. Knowing your user influences the way that you say things. If you're a professional speaker, for instance, your text should speak to the person who would hire you, such as meeting planners rather than the audience members.

Experts see things differently

Stanford Persuasive Technology Lab also ran a study on experts' perceptions of credibility. Experts in health and finance rated five pairs of Web sites in their fields. They were given 30 items, asked to rate how much each variable impacted the credibility of the site, and given an optional area to add comments. Interestingly, experts rated credibility very differently than consumers did. Here's how it broke down:

Health Experts' Ratings of Credibility
Name/reputation/affiliation: 43.9 percent
Information source: 25.8 percent
Company motive: 22.7 percent
Information focus: 19.7 percent
Advertising: 13.6 percent
Design look: 7.6 percent

Health experts were most impacted by the source of the information. For example, the Mayo Clinic site was viewed as highly credible. A strong sales focus hurt credibility, but a site could be for-profit without damaging credibility. Experts were wary of flashy design and strong (e.g., "proven") unsubstantiated language.

Finance Experts' Ratings of Credibility

Information focus: 40.3 percent
Company motive: 35.8 percent
Information bias: 29.9 percent
Design look: 16.4 percent
Information design: 13.4 percent
Name/reputation/affiliation: 10.5 percent

The most important aspect to the finance experts was the quality of information provided. They valued a breadth of unbiased information presented in a very clear manner. Like health experts, they were wary of flashy design and strong language.

Are you marketing to clients, experts, or both?

Be clear about the answer to this question as you meet new people. Depending on your target clients and referral partners, some may have greater subject matter expertise than others. Often referral partners are other professionals with expertise in your or a related field.

You may need to create different marketing materials for different audiences. David, a search engine optimization consultant, often received referrals from Web site coders and developers. These technical experts spoke a very different language from his clients, business owners who were looking for help being found on the Web. Because each audience would look for different information in determining whether or not David's site was credible, he created different mini-sites for different audiences. He determined that information focus would be important to both, but he varied the type of information provided for his technical colleagues who referred to him versus his clients.

Know Your Audience

ACTION STEPS

1. **Survey your audience.** The best way to discover what people value is to ask them. Create simple surveys that take people just a couple of minutes to answer.

2. **Create different sites for different audiences.** For example, if you're a homeopathic physician who specializes in working with children and your referral partners are other homeopathic physicians who work with adults only, you may have one site for these experts (with more detailed information, data, journal studies, references, and so on) and one site for the clients in your target market.

3. **Have different places within the same site for different audiences.** You can have a section of professional resources for experts. Or have people select which place to go for more information. This is similar to when you call a pharmacy and the recording says, "Press 1 if you are a physician calling in a prescription. Press 2 if you are a patient . . ."

4. **Be credible to both experts and clients.** If you will have one site that speaks to everyone, be sure to focus on the overall aesthetic and navigation, keeping it professional and not "flashy" or "salesy," which turns off experts. Keep the writing style understandable to the lay person, but provide footnotes with references for the experts.

Credibility and Your Brand

Your brand consists of everything that makes up your identity: your logo, tagline, Web site, headshot, name (both your name and your business name), office décor, and so on. When people experience your brand, they will have a psychological reaction that includes their thoughts, beliefs, attitudes, feelings, perceptions, images, attention, and memory. To be seen as credible, one of the first things your brand must feel is genuine.

The power of authenticity and brand consistency

A few months ago I met with a new client, a professional law practice, at their offices in one of the suburbs of Philadelphia. Before meeting with them, I was afraid that they might be stuffy people who lacked warmth. Imagery on their Web site included architectural columns that seemed to represent a Center City courthouse. Nothing about their brand made me excited to meet them or work with them. If the situation were reversed and I were a potential client for their law practice, I doubt that I would have become a client.

I drove up to their office and was surprised to find that it was a beautiful old stone building—a house from about 1920 that had been converted to offices. The entrance was flanked by large hydrangea bushes with big blue flowers. The windows had flowerboxes with draping purple petunias and lime green scrolling sweet potato vine. When I met three of the partners, they were instantly warm and personable. They seemed smart, but their personalities were inconsistent with the attorneys in buttoned up navy pinstriped suits that their Web site image portrayed.

"Okay, before we get to anything else, we've got to address your online branding," I started out by saying.

"Here you are in this beautiful location on Main Street. Many of your clients could walk here. You seem serious about your work but also seem like laid-back family-oriented people who care deeply about your immediate community. These are the things we need to emphasize in your branding. Instead, your Web site gives the appearance of a wannabe big-city corporate firm, something that you are not and should not be. There's nothing wrong with emphasizing the benefits that come with being a large, powerful, exclusive cosmopolitan firm *if* that's who you actually are. Your clients don't want this or they would be driving into the city and going to one of those firms."

We ended up making over not just their Web site but the unique selling proposition of their business, their personal styles, and their waiting area and offices to enhance their credibility and brand alignment. They attracted more ideal clients and developed relationships with other professionals. Perhaps most important, they had a greater sense of authenticity and realness. They *felt* more credible, which came across in all of their marketing.

The psychology of color and imagery

Color is one of the most powerful ways to influence the perception of you and your brand. Understanding how your audience responds to color enhances your credibility and likeability with them.

Toby Israel, an environmental psychologist and author of *Some Place Like Home: Using Design Psychology to Create Ideal Spaces*, gave The Myers-Briggs personality test to clients. The Myers-Briggs categorizes people on the basis of four dimensions: introvert/extrovert, intuiting/sensing, thinking/feeling, and judging/perceiving. Toby found that people who rated higher on the thinking dimension (versus feeling) preferred cooler colors and more modern styles in their designs, whereas people who rated higher on the feeling dimension preferred prefer warmer colors and wood.

If you see clients in your office, consider what kind of art to use and what color to paint your walls. These ideas can also be used for the design of your logo, colors, and selection of imagery to use on your Web site and in your social media branding. A 2009 study investigated whether personality features (using the "big five" personality domains: extroversion, agreeableness, conscientiousness, neuroticism, and openness) were related to preference for different types of art (including portraiture, abstract art, geometric art, and impressionism). Results from 3,254 participants showed that people who like abstract art tend to be sensation-seekers high on the openness personality domain. People high on openness tend to have a broad range of interests and active imaginations. If your clients are the types of people who like change, novelty, new experiences, and adventure, use artwork with abstract imagery. On the other hand, if these types of things are unsettling to your clients and they prefer stability and calm, then consider artwork with realistic imagery. This study also found that people who are extroverted enjoy art that has people or reminders of lots of people around. If you tend to work with actors, for example, the imagery on your Web site and in your office could include a lot of people. If, on the other hand, you tend to work with people who are more introverted, such as research scientists, you may not want to include imagery with a lot of people.

Another study found that brightly colored spaces such as red rooms created an excited state in the brain, which paradoxically lowered heart rates. Introverts and people already in a negative mood were more impacted than others, and their performance on tasks in these spaces suffered. People tended to report feeling more positive in red rooms than blue rooms, and essays they wrote in red rooms were more creative, but had more clerical errors.

Credibility and Your Brand

ACTION STEPS

1. **Choose photos that appeal to your audience**. Most of us select our headshot based on how flattering it is. Instead, the thing to focus on is the message that it conveys to your potential client. When I got my headshot done recently, I loved one of them. I decided to post three options on my page Facebook.com/MarketingPsych and ask people to vote. The one I liked best was the loser by far. Which did I choose? The favorite of my audience.

2. **Brand your social media pages.** Keep the colors consistent with your brand. Hire a graphic designer to create your Twitter background, sign-up boxes, and special announcements.

3. **Ask someone who knows you well to look over your marketing materials and say whether those materials feel like you.** Your professional brand may be a more polished version of you, but there should be a sense of authenticity and congruency among your brand elements and personality.

4. **Strike the balance between content and relationship.** When you post in social media, consider including messages that show your ideas as well as who you are. The best balance depends on your comfort level, professional dictates, and your audience. I tend to go for about 70 percent focused content (related to the psychology of marketing) and 30 percent relationship content (related to me personally).

5. **Strike the balance between content and promotion**. Too much promotion hurts your credibility. The right amount depends on your

market and also on the type of media in which your market. I feel that very little promotion should be done in social media, that it is more of a relationship-building tool and tends to favor a ratio of around 90 percent content and 10 percent promotion.

6. **Show your passion.** Don't be afraid to let your passion for the work you do and the clients you serve show. Don't let your professionalism kill you. Enthusiasm is contagious.

Establish Expertise

When you're the expert on your topic, you activate one of the most powerful social influence principles: authority. Dr. Robert B. Cialdini, founder of Influence at Work and author of the groundbreaking books *Influence: Science & Practice* and *Yes! 50 Scientifically Proven Ways to Be Persuasive*, includes "authority" as one of the six most powerful tools of social influence (along with reciprocation, commitment, social proof, liking, and scarcity, which we discuss in other chapters). Here's one example of the strength of authority.

In 1971, Philip Zimbardo, a professor of psychology at Stanford University, conducted one of the most illuminating social psychology studies in history, the Stanford prison experiment. Seventy college students in the United States and Canada answered a newspaper ad for the opportunity to earn $15 per day by participating in a study at Stanford. After screening for psychological or medical problems, 24 males were selected and randomly assigned to become a guard or a prisoner for two weeks in the basement of Stanford's psychology department building, which had been transformed to look and feel like a prison with bars on the doors and no windows. Prisoners entered in a state of shock after having been "arrested" by city police officers and brought to the prison blindfolded. They then experienced the humiliation of being strip-searched, deloused with a spray, and dressed in a smock with their number, shackles on their feet, and a stocking cap on their head. The guards wore identical khaki outfits, mirrored sunglasses, and carried billy clubs. The first day was fairly uneventful, but on the second day of the experiment, the prisoners revolted. They ripped off their stocking caps and numbers and cursed at the guards. The guards responded forcefully—they stripped the prisoners naked and put several into solitary confinement. Guards continued to use physical and psychological measures to keep prisoners in their place. One prisoner broke down on day three and was released, and the whole experiment ended after just six days instead of the planned two weeks because of the damaging psychological effects on both guards and prisoners. Prisoners followed the rules of the guards, who followed the perceived rules of their roles to keep prisoners in line. During the experiment, parents came to study but no one overtly objected or asked that their son be released. The reason for all of this obedience? Authority. Factors of authority included the clothes people wore, the fact that the study was conducted at Stanford University, and the way in which the guards acted.

The Stanford prison experiment shows us just how powerful authority is. In this study, the harmful effects of abusing authority are clear. On the flip side, we can positively influence people by using authority. As with any tool of social influence, the effects are powerful, and we must carefully consider our ethical, legal, and moral values with the goal of influencing people for the better. So what are some of the ways in which we can convey authority to show credibility and positively influence others?

Know everything about your topic and provide exceptional value

When you're an expert in your field, you have a greater level of confidence and authority. You know that you're up on the latest research and ways to help your client, and your client receives exceptional value.

Neuroscience research shows that people's brains actually respond differently when the person speaking with them is an expert. In one study, when the communicator was an expert, functional magnetic resonance imaging showed activity in the prefrontal and temporal cortices, which involve active processing and elaboration. Expert communicators also affected the caudate nucleus and people's attitudes of trustworthiness, learning, reward, and value. In addition, people perceived as experts impacted the medial temporal lobe and enhanced memory. Our brains, therefore, recognize, trust, and remember experts better than others.

When you're the expert in your field, you have immediate credibility. You're able to refer to what you've learned at recent trainings, in books you've read, by helping other clients, and in your formal education. Clients and potential referral partners feel relaxed and comfortable with you. They feel like you "know your stuff." It is typically not possible to be and be perceived as the expert if your scope is too large. Instead, own a narrow area of your field and be the best in the world at that.

In general, titles and degrees are a quick and effective way to show your expertise. While using your titles is often helpful, remember the prison experiment and think about how much power you want to have. Sometimes leading with your title can intimidate other people and reduce their comfort, creativity, or confidence to challenge you.

You may have continuing education requirements in your field, but consider going beyond these on a quest for ongoing knowledge and expertise. Think about what your client would perceive as conveying expertise—it may be that a particular training, certification, or study is not of value to them, but that there is something else that is.

Be polished and professional without being too polished and professional

Numerous studies show how much more credibility and influence people in uniforms have than people in lay clothes. You may have noticed how doctors often wear scrubs or white coats on television, which commands an instant level of attention and respect. Your clothes may place you in a power position over other people. Or you may choose to dress similarly to your clients and potential referral partners if it makes sense to equalize the perception of power. One of my clients told me that in her field in medicine, dressing well conveyed a level of respect for patients. I had never thought of it in this way, but dressing well can connote, "You're worth it," while dressing very casually can indicate, "I can't be bothered."

Accessories such as handbags, watches, other jewelry, and even cars send an important message as well. Your clients and potential referral partners will feel most comfortable when these trappings indicate that you are successful. Everyone wants to work with the person who's the best and most successful. On the other hand, if you overdo the prestige and affluence indicators, people may wonder if they are just "little fish" to you and if you'll give them the attention that they need. They may perceive you as materialistic and feel uncomfortable. The culture in which you live, the client's background, and many other factors come into play in determining where the happy medium lies. One of my friends in Los Angeles told me of the expression, "You can never be too rich or too skinny." In many areas and situations, however, being seen as too rich, too skinny, too polished, and so on can be a bad thing.

Someone may come across as beautifully polished but may have the air of a beauty pageant contestant and lack credibility. Someone may dress professionally but lack a sense of style and personality. In considering your choices for clothing and accessories, emphasize congruence with your brand. Your expertise, tone of voice, personality, body language, color choices, style, and so on should all fit together like a seamless puzzle. All of these things are part of nonverbal communication. If there is a mismatch between your verbal and nonverbal communication, people believe the nonverbal.

Establish Expertise

ACTION STEPS

1. **Be the speaker.** Instead of attending networking events, elevate your authority by being the speaker. Not only will you be able to share your ideas with everyone, but you will be more influential when you are the expert.

2. **Commit to your continuing education program.** Plan how you can receive ongoing training and education so you are on the cutting edge in your field. Your confidence will increase, your clients will receive the best possible service, and your expert status will be enhanced.

3. **Provide valuable content on a regular basis.** This is the rule for all things marketing, including your Web site or blog. If there is breadth of content, be sure that it fits together. If the content is narrow, be sure that you provide enough to give useful information and keep people coming

back. Think of your blog or Web site like a plant. The content is the water that helps it survive and thrive. A good rule of thumb is to add content every day or every other day.

4. **Lead with your most important stuff.** You wouldn't believe how often I find people's key credentials buried in their bios rather than featured up front. Include affiliations that have name recognition, such as professional associations.

5. **Build your platform.** Find more resources on building your platform and establishing yourself as the go-to expert in your field at my site PlatformBuildingCenter.com.

Now that we've discussed the four powerful ways to initiate relationships in the first four chapters, let's move on to the next section and explore how to follow up, add ongoing value, stimulate discussions, and be memorable.

Part 2

How Do I Create Meaningful Connections That Last?

Chapter 5

Be Memorable—
People Can Be Aware of Only
a Few Things at a Time

I am a total believer of making the process a good time—make it
memorable, have some fun, try to shoot high in your quality and
then don't get crazy, see what happens.

—*GARRY MARSHALL*

YOU ARE NOT the first thing on people's minds. No offense, it's just that
everyone has a lot on their minds each day.

Think about the last couple business contacts you made but have not
regularly heard from. Were they on your mind today? If not, it is because
you are human and have many other things on your mind. The same
holds true for your business contacts. This is why follow-up is so important—so people don't forget about you. In this chapter, I'll give you a quick
primer on how memory works and what is and what isn't memorable. In
the other chapters in this section, we'll discuss specific ways to keep in
touch with people and jog their memory.

How Do You Get into Memory?

As you know, there are millions of things competing for our attention every day. In order for someone to remember you, they must first pay attention to you. It can be challenging to grab someone's attention, much less get into their memory. We discussed ways to command attention in Chapter 2. Once you have successfully directed someone's focus and attention at you, you have a brief period of time to get into memory.

Let's begin with a quick overview of how memories work. Memories work like files in a filing cabinet. A memory involves three primary ingredients: First, information is encoded (put into memory). This is like opening the drawer of the filing cabinet. Second, information is stored in memory. This is like creating and labeling a file for the memory and putting it into the filing cabinet. Third, the memory is retrieved. Without this step, that file will stay in the filing cabinet, unable to be accessed. Retrieval is taking the file out of the filing cabinet at the appropriate time.

Step 1: Encoding new information

In order for new information to be encoded into memory, the first step of the memory creation process, it must

1. Be attended to
2. Go into short-term memory
3. Go into long-term memory (often via working memory)

We've already discussed #1, how to get attention, in Chapter 2. Once something comes into our awareness via our senses (taste, touch, smell, sound, sight) and we put our attention on something, it lasts there for a very brief period of time, typically under one second. The information then goes on to our short-term memory where it can last for about 10 to 15 seconds if it isn't acted on.

Let's say, for example, that I asked you to remember a string of letters: A, C, X, F, D. You would probably be able to hold these letters in your short-term memory for about 10 seconds without rehearsing them.

Step 2: Storing new information

How much can we hold in short-term memory? You may have heard the magic number 7 +/- 2 for how many pieces of information (5 to 9) we can remember in the short term.

The concept of passive maintenance of information in short-term memory has been expanded to include working memory, which involves the active manipulation of information. Without working memory, things can go "in one ear and out the other." Working memory helps them to stick. It does so by rehearsing or otherwise working with information. If, for example, I asked you to tell me that same list of letters backwards I gave you earlier (A, C, X, F, D), you would involve your working memory because you'd be manipulating the information. Working memory can serve to facilitate memories moving from short-term to long-term memory. When people work with information rather than just try to hold it in their minds, they are more likely to remember it. Think back to when you were in school—when you talked through information, integrated it with knowledge you already had, or made flash cards, you would remember it better than if you just read it and tried to remember it. If you have a school-aged child, you can help her study in this active way to improve her retention of information.

Many things can impact the functioning of our working memory. When I was in graduate school, my dissertation explored the impact of mood. I administered and scored a battery of neuropsychological tests with 100 participants. The results indicated that the mood that people were in when they took the tests significantly impacted their working memory. People who were in a depressed mood had much more difficulty remembering information, especially complex information presented visually. This means that if someone is anxious or depressed at the time you present new information to them, they may be less likely to remember it.

Working memory is a very important concept for your marketing efforts because once information is manipulated in working memory, it is more likely to be remembered. All of the tips in this chapter and the three that follow are designed to get people's working memory systems involved so you'll be memorable. One of my clients, Omar, a salesperson in communication technologies, told me that he had no luck with net-working. He met people, but when he went to follow up with them, they didn't know who he was. This was embarrassing and no fun for him, so he stopped networking. Together we worked on his branding so that he'd stand out as unique. He had a great memorable background story that people could relate to. When he told his story, it made people think of some of their own experiences. They were integrating the new information about Omar with their existing knowledge base, which activates working memory. When Omar made follow-up calls, people almost always remembered him.

Once information is manipulated, rehearsed, or associated with other thoughts, it goes into your long-term memory. As the name implies, long-term memory lasts for a long time, which can be days or decades.

- What was the name of your third grade teacher?
- What did you have for dinner last night?
- What was your favorite vacation you've been on?
- What was your high school graduation like?

It takes your long-term memory to answer any of these questions.

Step 3: Retrieving information

The final step in creating a memory is retrieving it. You can go through the process of getting attention, getting into short-term memory, and getting into long-term memory, but if people don't access these memories, nothing will happen. It's like you've earned money (gotten into memory) but can't spend it because it's in a vault and you've lost the key.

There are essentially two ways of retrieving information from memory—it can be recognized or recalled. Recognition memory is nice because it doesn't require a ton of effort from people. If I gave you a list of four objects—ball, book, phone, cup—and then asked you which of the following objects was on the original list—plane, pen, phone, or frame—you would recognize "phone" as being on the list. Multiple choice questions often make use of recognition memory because you need only to spot the correct answer. Your personal brand facilitates recognition memory. Your name may be enough for someone to recognize you, or your face, or your company name, or a story that you told. If your image is easily recognized, you could call someone and say, "This is Dave Smith, the guy in the bright green suit from the other night." If you compare yourself to someone, however, there should be a mild self-deprecating element; for example, you don't want to say, "This is Rachel, the one who looks like the supermodel Heidi Klum."

The second type of memory retrieval is recall. Recall memory can be free or cued. Free recall is the ability to remember items without much framework. For example, if I asked you to list all of the presenters from a conference, your response would show free recall of the names. If you're like most people, you'd be able to come up with around five names. Free recall is not ideal to use in marketing because it requires the most amount of effort from someone. We have to really think to come up with the responses.

When people remember something without cues, they often remember a situation in order, which is called serial recall. The serial positioning effect comes into play because we tend to remember items at the beginning or at the end of a sequence best, forgetting what's in the middle.

Cued recall is similar to free recall but you are given cues. If I said, "Who was the female presenter with the short dark hair who spoke about mistakes in wealth management?" your response would show cued recall of her name. Cued recall is typically less effortful than free recall because it gives someone a framework within which to think.

How Do You Get into Memory?

ACTION STEPS

1. **Ask compelling questions.** A great way to stimulate working memory is to ask questions. If you're speaking before an audience, you may ask questions for people to answer out loud or questions people can answer in their heads. Either way, getting them to take action on the information you provide stimulates working memory and helps you get into long-term memory.

2. **Know your mental file.** If someone already has a file or framework for what you do, how you can help them, or how you can work with them, it will be easier for them to remember you. Consider what file someone would put you in.

3. **Within the general file, you want to have your own unique folder.** If you're unique enough, you can create your own mental file in people's minds. Imagine that someone took out the folder and labeled it for you— what would it say? Your unique selling proposition may include what you do, who you work with, how you work with them, or any other aspect of your business that is different and can be a file in someone's memory. Don't let yourself be filed under "Other" or "Miscellaneous."

Make Yourself Memorable

Now that you're familiar with how memories are created, stored, and retrieved, we can explore ways to make sure that you are memorable.

Build relationships but keep them simple

As we've discussed, working memory involves the ability to create mental relationships between different things. Australian researchers from the University of Queensland gave people a sentence like the following:

> If the cake is from France, then it has more sugar if it is made with chocolate than if it is made with cream, but if the cake is from Italy, then it has more sugar if it is made with cream than if it is made of chocolate.

They asked people to remember the relationships between the different types of cake, country, and sugar content.

Most people could remember statements like this one that had a three-way interaction (country, ingredient, sugar). When the researchers introduced a four-way interaction, a significant decline in accuracy was observed, and five-way interactions produced an accuracy level the same as chance or guessing.

Creating relationships between things gets people involved and helps them to form a memory. What can you create relationships between? Ideally between you (or your services) and other things of interest to your audience. For example, one client, an attorney with a midsized firm in New York City, wrote a series of articles and blog posts that related his services to sports because he and many of his clients were sports enthusiasts.

Remind people of themselves (or those they love)

As you create relationships in your marketing communications, consider how to remind people of themselves. Brain studies reveal some interesting things about how we remember things connected to ourselves. Dartmouth College researchers recruited 24 participants ages 18 to 30 and set them up with functional magnetic resonance imaging (fMRI) to measure their brain activity. The participants' brains were imaged while they made judgments about adjectives on a computer screen. The adjectives were about themselves (they were asked, "Does this adjective describe you?"), someone else (a political figure—"Does this adjective describe the current U.S. president?"), or the case of the letters ("Is this adjective printed in upper-case letters?"). An adjective, such as "polite," would appear on the screen along with a cue word (self, president, or case) for just 2000 milliseconds.

When their memories were tested, it was clear that they remembered the words that they related to themselves the best. In fact, the fMRI results showed that memories about themselves activated a different part of their brains. In general, the relevance judgments (self or president) activated a different part of the brain (the left inferior frontal cortex and the anterior cingulate) compared with the case judgments. In addition, the self judgments activated a separate region of the medial prefrontal cortex.

This means that we process information that we view as relevant to ourselves differently on a neurocognitive level than we process other information. Studies have shown that this powerful self-referential effect is reduced if the judgments about others are for those we are closely connected to, such as our family members or good friends.

So to be memorable, you want to draw connections between your business and things that people associate with themselves. And if not themselves, then things that they associate with people who they are closely connected to. You'll need to know some information about the person with whom you're connecting to make this work, so the first step is to ask questions to find out what people associate with themselves. For instance, one of my clients, a communications coach, made it her goal to find out something important that she had in common with the person she was networking with. By asking questions and listening carefully to the answers, she was able to draw connections and even explain her services in a way the person would understand and remember. If she found out that someone was into horseback riding, when explaining her services she would say, "You know how with horseback riding you need to first learn how to walk and stop before learning to trot, then canter, and then jump? That is exactly what I help my clients to do in their presentations."

Stand out

There are a few more things that you can do to increase the likelihood of going from short-term memory into long-term memory. One is known as the Von Restorff effect, which essentially means that when things are presented together, whatever stands out the most would be remembered better than the others. You can use the visual aids we discussed in Chapter 2 (color, form, luminance) or informational aids, such an intriguing story or something else that is remarkable and therefore memorable about you.

Imagine that you're at a networking event and consider how other people will present themselves. What can you do so that you will stand out and be more memorable than the others? It does not have to be something dramatic. Because communication is more about how we say something than what we say, don't put too much pressure on yourself to say something remarkable and intriguing. It may be that you have excellent listening skills and make someone feel that you're curious and interested to learn more about them. A memory can be a feeling, so if you pair yourself with that positive feeling, you're much more likely to be remembered.

One of my favorite ways to stand out is to give a creative demonstration of what you do. You can do this by using a visual object as a metaphor for you or your services. For example, one of my clients used fruit salad as a metaphor for his service (each fruit represented a component) during a presentation. He put together the fruit salad as he spoke and the audience had an awesome visual—and tasty treat. Food always helps, and when you give people something you activate the law of reciprocity, which we'll discuss in Chapter 10.

Go first

Another memory trick involves the position in which things are presented. This is called the serial positioning effect, with items being remembered more if they are presented in the first or the last part of the sequence.

There is some evidence that the first position is remembered even better than the last. Research on ad placements during the 2006 Super Bowl showed that the first ads were remembered best. If you were going to speak on a panel, you'd want to be the first or the last speaker. Going first may be the last thing you want to do, so remember this data because it can be worth it. Even though you may want to wait to introduce yourself at the networking event or speak on a panel, go first to be best remembered. Going first can also reduce speaking anxiety because you don't have time for your anxious anticipation to build and to compare yourself with others. So go first to reduce anxiety and improve memorability.

Break up information

Another useful memory device is called "chunking." This involves pairing similar objects together. Since most people can work with around five pieces of information, if you have more, you want to group them. Consider how the telephone number (555) 555-5555 is more memorable than 5555555555.

You can use this strategy on your Web site by including lists of bullets. (Pop quiz: How many items do you want to have on a list of bullets so people pay attention and remember them? Ideally less than five and definitely no more than seven.) You can also break up text into boxes that fit together but are visually distinct. (Again, how many boxes of text do you want to have? Yup, no more than five.)

Make Yourself Memorable

ACTION STEPS

1. **Relate yourself to other things.** Our memory systems are like filing cabinets. Get into existing files by relating to other things. For example, a financial advisor may say to someone, "You know how a car goes dramatically down in value the minute it's driven off a dealer's lot? I help people figure out when it's smart to buy a new car versus a used car and all those other important financial decisions we need to make."

2. **Help people associate your services with themselves.** We best remember those things that remind us of ourselves. The area in which you relate to someone may be professional or personal. It may be that you are both avid scuba divers who have recently done the Great Barrier Reef, or you're both lovers of Tibetan Terriers. Or it may be something about your services that is similar to theirs. My business associates who I respect and think of often are similar to me in the value they place on research-based marketing principles and anti-guru ("Do this because it worked for me") approaches.

3. **Ask yourself, "What would I remember about me?"** Be clear and strategic about how you would stand out from others who your contacts meet with.

4. **Go first or last, ideally first.** We tend to remember information best that is presented first or last. Whenever you meet people or present, take the opportunity to go first. You might not want to, but it will pay off.

5. **Package information together.** Keep information sorted into small chunks of three to five pieces. Let's say that you want to write a blog post, "The Top 10 Ways to Be Memorable." Consider breaking your information up into several blog posts to help people remember points 1 to 3, then 4 to 7, then 8 to 10. Better yet, change your topic to "The Top 6 Ways to Be Memorable," and people will be likely to remember them all.

Now Get Recognized

Now that you've successfully captured attention and used working memory to create a memory file for you in long-term memory, which can last hours or decades, we need to help people access that memory.

Getting into memory is challenging, but unfortunately, as soon as you're there, the process of forgetting begins. Don't take it personally, it's just how our minds work.

To make sure that your business is not forgettable, we need to help people remember you. The type of memory that is involved here is recognition memory (as opposed to free recall, where people would have to think of you on their own). Recognition memory tends to take less effort and be easier for people than free or cued recall, so let's focus our efforts on being recognized.

There are two important processes associated with recognition memory:

- Recalling you within particular context
- Being familiar with you

To get at the first, let's say that you were e-mailing a potential joint venture partner who you met at a conference a couple of years ago. You could say, "I met you at the Internet marketing conference in Philadelphia in July 2010 and really enjoyed discussing your theories about digital media over lunch."

Something I like to do is to take photos of myself with people who I meet in person. I then attach the photos to the e-mail to help them remember who I am. Since we tend to be better at remembering faces than names, this is a great recognition aid.

To get at the second (being familiar with you), you want to stay in touch with people on a fairly regular basis to keep your familiarity alive. We'll discuss how to do this in the next two chapters.

It is *your* responsibility to make sure that people remember you. Don't assume that they do because if they don't, they will feel stupid, and the last thing you want to do is make your potential clients or referral partners feel stupid.

Now Get Recognized

ACTION STEPS

1. **Remind people of a salient experience.** Don't assume that someone remembers you; rather, describe the context in which they met or worked with you.

2. **Expect that people won't remember.** Don't feel bad if someone doesn't remember you or make them feel bad for not remembering you. You'll come across as arrogant and entitled. Instead, compliment their memory of you: "You must have met 100 people at that event. I'm flattered that you remember me." Of course, you've done some work to make that happen, but remain humble and take the opportunity to pay a compliment—that person deserves it for having been present and paying attention when she could have been thinking of a million other things.

3. **Send a photo** or other way for people to remember you, especially if you have a name like John Smith that is not particularly unique.

4. **Stay in touch so people don't forget you.** Mental memory files get moved back further and further until they no longer exist. Keep yours in front by staying in touch. (More tips on this in the next chapter.)

Now you know how important it is to follow up. Of course, you probably already knew this. But are you doing it regularly? If not, you're like just about everyone else who doesn't have the time, system, or fresh ideas for how to follow up. Let's get into that now.

Chapter 6

Follow Up—
People Are Comforted
by Consistency

We are what we repeatedly do. Excellence, therefore, is not an
act but a habit.

—ARISTOTLE

A COUPLE OF weeks ago, I attended an excellent networking event. The best part was chatting with people, many of whom were excellent connections for my business. I typically follow up right away after meeting people and have developed many of my best professional relationships this way. This time, however, I decided to conduct an experiment: I decided to wait and see what would happen if I did not follow up. I had 10 cards on my desk from people who had expressed significant interest in staying in touch with me. Yet after a week, not one of them had. No one had followed up.

Are you similarly guilty of not following up when you should?

Do you have a stack of business cards on your desk, just sitting there?

Do you struggle with finding the right mix of keeping in touch but not becoming pushy or annoying?

If you answered yes to any of these three questions, you need to develop a better system for keeping in touch. *System* is the key word because you don't want to reinvent the wheel each time you need to follow up. You don't want to have to put a ton of thought into each follow-up, or chances are good that you will not take action. You'll decide that you don't have enough time and won't do anything.

The Problem of Inconsistent Follow-Up

The other day, one of my clients, Steven, a consultant who connects companies with financing for major projects and improvements, admitted that he has been lax about following up with his partners. His partners tend to be the companies that provide the improvement services—contractors, construction companies, appliance companies, and the like. He said to me, "I think I should send out an e-mail or a flyer or something."

"Steven," I said, "what is the first thing that you think when you receive a piece of marketing from a company you haven't heard from in a long time?"

"That they're hard up for business."

"Exactly."

What he needed to do was not to send out an e-mail when his business slowed down, but instead to create a keep-in-touch strategy and system. When you don't have a *regular* keep-in-touch system in place, you will look like you need or want something when you do keep in touch. And it will probably be true. You'll think to follow up only when you need business. Then when you follow up, it may come across negatively, as in Steven's example. Or you won't do it for fear of coming across negatively. Or you'll do it but you won't feel good about it and won't get the results you want.

In contrast, when people are used to regularly receiving high-quality content and information from you, three important things happen:

- You build trust and further your relationship with them.
- They see your keep-in-touch as providing value rather than as trying to sell something.
- They don't mind when you occasionally do try to sell something.

We need to, therefore, create a strategy and a plan for staying in touch with your prospective and current partners and clients on a regular basis.

The Problem of Inconsistent Follow-Up

ACTION STEPS

1. **Review your follow-up system over the past 12 months.** Did you neglect to follow up on new or existing connections? Did you make the mistake of following up only when you needed new business?

2. **Figure out why you didn't follow up.** Avoidance is usually driven by fear. Ask yourself if you were afraid of any of the following:

   Rejection

   Wasting your time

   Wasting someone else's time

   Being seen as pushy or salesy

   Not saying the right thing

   Not knowing what to say

   Ruining a positive first impression you had made

   Something else?

3. **Overcome the fear.** If you discover that a fear listed above or another prevents you from following up, ask yourself, "What's the worst thing that can happen?" Remember that the only failure is not to try, and if

you don't ask, the answer's always no. Commit to using the tools in this chapter to follow up more regularly so you can overcome your fear by learning that it is unlikely to come true.

4. **Review your systems.** Sometimes people don't fear or worry about anything related to following up but don't do it because they're not organized and don't have a system in place. It takes a lot of time and energy to reinvent the wheel each time, so most people won't do anything if they don't have a system. Do you have an effective system in place? If not, keep reading.

The Magic Recipe

My recipe for follow-up that leads to great results is:

System + Timing + Value + Personalization = Great Follow-Up

The first two variables, system and timing, address how you follow up. The second two, value and personalization, address what you will do to follow up. We'll focus on the systems and timing in this chapter and value and personalization in the next chapter to examine unique ways to provide value in your keep-in-touch marketing.

What's your system?

You may need a few different systems, depending on your marketing funnels and your audiences. Your marketing funnel is the process by which someone comes into contact with you until they hire you. Let's say that you're a consultant and you have two marketing funnels, one for your potential clients, and one for your potential strategic referral partners. For example:

Client Marketing Funnel
1. Client finds you through search engine
2. Client comes onto your Web site

3. Client wants a freebie you offer and signs up for your e-mail mailing list
4. Client receives your twice-monthly value-packed electronic newsletter
5. Client responds to a promotion in your newsletter for a discounted first session
6. Client completes first session and enrolls in additional consulting

Referrals Marketing Funnel
1. Call potential strategic referral partner (PSRP)
2. Meet PSRP for lunch
3. Keep in touch once monthly with PSRP by sending articles, etc.
4. Send thank-you letter when referral is received
5. Meet with referral partner quarterly to further the relationship

You may have a couple marketing funnels for each type of marketing that you do. The client marketing funnel above is primarily Internet marketing. If you speak or network, you may need a separate marketing funnel for those.

Once you're clear on your funnel, you can ask yourself what systems you need, such as what contact management systems for e-mail marketing. Be clear on what specifications you need before committing to a system, and take advantage of the free trial offers. I made the mistake of building an e-mail list of over 10,000 in one contact management system only to learn that they did not offer a key feature I needed (autoresponders). So I had to move my list, which resulted in loss of many subscribers. Invest the time, energy, and money (you may need to hire a consultant to help you make the decisions) up front to do your research and save time, energy, and money down the line.

Follow up without hounding people

In determining the timing of your follow-up, the first topic to address is when you will follow up after an initial meeting. My rule of thumb is that the more personal the meeting, the more time you have—but you still don't have much time. If you have a personal interaction, such as meeting someone at a networking event, I believe you have a couple of days to follow up. Definitely no more than a week. If you have an impersonal interaction, such as a social media connection or someone signing up for your newsletter, I believe you have minutes. You'll want to use e-mail contact management software that automatically responds when someone signs up for your newsletter or free giveaway.

The second topic is how often you will contact people. There are two important considerations: how much time you have to create quality content and how often people in your target market like to be contacted.

As we will discuss in the next chapter, it is critical that the information you share in your follow-up is valuable. The idea put forth by marketing visionary Seth Godin in *Permission Marketing* is that you want to be in touch with people by providing value rather than interruption. In general, advertising is not particularly effective for service professionals. A service is a relationship, and it needs to be mutually beneficial. That said, we need to consider carefully how much time you can invest in creating beneficial information to share in your follow-up. Creating content typically takes longer than we think it will, so be conservative in estimating the time necessary. It can become an issue of quantity versus quality. We need to be in contact with people enough so that we are not forgettable (at least once per month in most markets, typically once per week or once every other week), but it may be impossible to write an article or create extensive content every week.

Also consider your personality. Do you get overwhelmed or intimidated when sitting down to create a polished video, audio, or article? Do you tend to think and communicate in quick blurbs? If so, you may prefer to use social media such as Twitter or your Facebook page to follow up. Are you a perfectionist who wants to make sure that everything you put out is of the highest caliber? If so, you may do better with writing a once-per-week compelling blog post and not using something like Twitter. If you tried to make every tweet perfect, it would take up way too much time, and it isn't necessary since tweets are fleeting and so brief that you can't possibly convey a great deal of information. You can, however, integrate Twitter with your blog so announcements of your captivating blog posts go out. For example, Daniel, a thoughtful, introverted therapist with a tinge of perfectionism, felt that he had to be selective and professional about what he put out on the Web. So he kept his keep-in-touch strategy very simple by posting high-quality articles on his blog and sending them to those on his mailing list once per week. He integrated his blog with his Twitter account, Facebook page, and LinkedIn profile so that even those who were not on his mailing list would receive updates with links to his articles. Because his articles were so thought-provoking, people often retweeted his article posts and inquired about reprinting his articles, furthering his exposure.

The other consideration is the person with whom you're staying in touch. How often do they like to be contacted? This can be hard to determine, but you can come up with an estimate by

- **Seeing how often they keep in touch** (send out their newsletter, etc.) themselves.
- **Thinking about what type of professional they are.** In general, people who are active with Internet marketing are used to getting a lot of e-mails and would be okay with more frequent e-mail communication.
- **Tracking your e-mail sign-ups and opt-outs.** If you are getting a lot of opt-outs after you have sent several communications out close together, you may be sending too much for those in your audience.
- **Asking yourself what you prefer if you are a member of that group yourself.** If you are a psychologist and your keep-in-touch marketing is going to other psychologists, you can use yourself and a few peers as a gauge.

Weighing the amount of time you have, how long it takes you to create excellent content, how often you could create content without having the quality suffer, your personality, and how your prospects like to be contacted should help you create your timing strategy. Once you have your strategy, stick to it no matter what. I've had several clients admit, "When I'm busy, I don't follow up with people, and then when I'm slow, I'm sorry that I didn't." Consistently follow up while it's raining business *and* when you're in a drought. This consistent follow-up will help prevent the downpours and droughts by bringing in consistent business.

The Magic Recipe

ACTION STEPS

1. **Write a list of everything that you need a system for,** such as:

   Keeping track of business cards

   Keeping track of when you follow up

   Keeping track of results of follow-up

   Sending out e-mail newsletters

   Sending out thank-you cards

2. **Create and polish your systems from step 1 above.** Ask friends and colleagues what systems they use. Experiment a bit to see what works well for you. Give yourself 60 days to experiment with your systems and then set them in stone, automating as much as possible.

3. **Do what you do best and outsource the rest.** Hire an assistant or organizer so you can focus on creating quality content and not on the logistics of setting up and sending everything. Virtual assistants are plentiful and typically charge between $15 to $75 an hour depending on the type of work they will do for you. If you have several virtual assistants, you may want to consider hiring a virtual manager. Look for someone who has completed the Online Business Manager (OBM) training with Tina Forsyth, or find an OBM on her site OnlineBusinessManager.com.

4. **Determine how often you will send out content and what works best to create it.** If you decide to send out an e-mail newsletter twice a month, for example, you will need to create a good amount of content. Do you work best in small chunks, or do you need to schedule half a day per month to do this?

The Trust Factor

We choose to do business with those whom we can trust. We may have times when we are misguided by a profitable opportunity and choose to do business with someone we're not sure if we can trust, and this usually turns out badly. Think of your follow-up systems as a way to build relationships and build trust over time.

What makes people see you as trustworthy?

In a 2006 article in the *Harvard Business Review*, Fordham University Professor of Management Robert F. Hurley lays out a trust model based on characteristics of both the truster and the situation or trustee:

Characteristics of the Truster
- **Risk tolerance.** Greater risk tolerance is associated with greater levels of trust. Risk takers tend to act first without extensive analysis. People who are more risk adverse often don't trust themselves in making decisions and take longer to trust others.
- **Adjustment.** People who are well adjusted, confident, and happy tend to see the world as trustworthy. People who are less well adjusted may be hypervigilant, suspicious, nervous, and less trusting. They may micromanage others.
- **Relative power.** Someone who has power or authority is more likely to trust, perhaps because they can penalize someone who betrays trust. If you feel you have less power, you are less likely to trust others.

Characteristics of the Situation or Trustee
- **Security.** People tend to ask themselves, "What's the worst thing that could happen?" If the answer is something that feels manageable, security goes up. Higher stakes situations lead to reduced security and less trust.
- **Similarities.** We tend to trust those who are like ourselves. Similarities may include having like values, being part of a shared group (such as alumni of the same university), sharing

a style of dress, or having in common other demographic or psychographic variables.

- **Alignment of interest.** We tend to trust those who have goals that are in alignment with ours. It is common to assume that parties have aligned interests, but these assumptions must be checked out because it is not always the case that they are aligned.
- **Benevolent concern.** This means that we feel that the other person has our best interests at heart. It can be a challenge if interests are competing.
- **Capability.** The more competence and expertise someone has, the more we trust them.
- **Predictability and integrity.** Does the other person feel confident that you will do what you say you will do when you say you will do it?
- **Quality of communication.** Do they perceive your communication style as open and honest?

In 2007, researchers F. David Schoorman, Roger C. Mayer, and James H. Davis reevaluated a seminal model of trust they developed in 1995. Their model draws from management, psychology, philosophy, and economics to create an integrative model for what creates trust in business relationships. Trust, they explain, is an aspect of relationships and includes people's perceptions about integrity, ability, and benevolence (i.e., how much someone wants to do good and not simply enhance their own profits). It is interesting to consider trust between individuals versus organizations. Because companies exist to increase profits, the benevolence motive may not be as strong between organizations as it may between individuals, such as sole proprietors or professionals in private practice. Regardless of whether the relationships are between individuals or organizations, the researchers propose that acting in a benevolent way when exploring options for joint venture partnerships builds trust. Judgments of someone's ability and integrity are likely to be created quickly, whereas judgments of benevolence may take more time.

Another factor that goes into trust is someone's willingness to take risks. If power is unbalanced in a relationship, the person who perceives herself as having more power is likely to take more risks. Finally, they propose that we form impressions of trust not simply by assessments (of ability, integrity, benevolence, and risk), which are cognitive factors, but also by our emotional response. As we discussed in Chapter 3, we often have an instant emotional reaction to something or someone. Trust seems to develop differently, however; the emotional reaction develops over time. Researchers Dunn and Schweitzer found that someone's emotional state at the time impacts how much they trust someone, even when that emotional state has nothing to do with the other person or the situation.

In one study, 78 teams of 3 to 4 undergraduate students each were tracked over 10 weeks. The students completed surveys including measures of familiarity, trust, how often they interacted, citizenship behaviors (such as how willingly they helped each other), the need to monitor each other, and performance. Early on, it was found, trust was one-dimensional (residing within an individual), and as time went on, it became two-dimensional (based on the relationship). This means that time is an important component of trust building. You must stay in touch with people over an extended period of time in order to build trust with them.

Cognitive and emotional trust emerged as separate variables that were built over time. The frequency of interaction was not related to trust. Consider this as you weigh the quantity versus quality dilemma that we discussed earlier—quality may be more important than quantity. Quality of interactions was not examined in this study.

Monitoring behaviors negatively impacted cognitive trust but not emotional trust. Team performance positively impacted emotional trust but not cognitive trust. Other factors that were positively related to trust included familiarity and citizenship behaviors. So the more that someone knows you and the more they feel that you do things to help them out, the more they will trust you. This is related to the familiarity principle called *propinquity*.

The power of propinquity

Just after World War II, Leon Festinger and his colleagues Stanley Schachter and Kurt Back conducted a classic social psychology experiment. They looked at married veteran students who were living in a new housing development at MIT, the Westgate apartments, to see how social groups or friendships developed. The friendships were based on spatial proximity or propinquity with most friendships between next door neigh-bors. Friendships between floors were related to proximity to staircases. The students in the study were a homogenous group, and in more hetero-geneous groups, propinquity may be shadowed by similarity effects (i.e., "birds of a feather flock together"). The propinquity effect is related to the mere exposure effect, which states that the more exposure we have to something, the more we like it. One study showed that people rated academic journals that they were more familiar with as having contrib-uted more to the field than journals with which they were less familiar. If, however, we do not like someone, repeated exposure can intensify our feelings of dislike. Familiarity, therefore, can intensify the dominant emo-tion someone experiences. Additionally, recent research has shown that the relationship between familiarity and liking goes both ways—liking can increase our perception of familiarity, and familiarity can increase our perception of liking.

While familiarity can enhance relationships, it may not play a posi-tive role when it comes to the reputation of a company or a brand. Some research has shown that familiarity with a company from presence in the media was negatively associated with reputation ratings (regardless of whether the media exposure was positive or negative). Margaret E. Brooks and Scott Highhouse review research that supports the idea that greater familiarity with a company is associated with mixed emotions and ambiva-lence about a company. Perhaps this is because the more familiar you are with something, the more associations—both positive and negative—come up. The feelings that are primary in a situation may depend on how someone was asked. For example, companies like Microsoft and Disney tend to come up high in polls of both worst and best companies. If com-panies are associated with both positive and negative thoughts, it may be that behaviors trigger one of the feelings. For example, behaviors viewed more favorably trigger the positive associations.

If familiarity is not necessarily related to our ratings of a brand's reputation, what is? There are many factors, but one that emerged in an interesting study is company culture. In this study, both culture and repu-tation were positively related to financial performance. A strong corporate culture provides a framework for employees' perceptions of the company's identity, which provides a sense of mission and collaboration. This can help people to work together and provide more valuable services to clients, which improves the reputation of the company.

The Trust Factor

ACTION STEPS

1. **Keep people in the loop.** It's a common scenario: You get a referral and are happy and thankful to the referral source. You get busy working with your new client, weeks go by, and you haven't been in touch with the referral source. We must have communication to have trust. Instead of falling into a cycle like this one, get in touch with the person who made the referral as soon as possible and let them know that you've scheduled the client, will provide a referral for the client, or whatever your plan is. If it will be several weeks before you can schedule the client, don't wait to let the referral provider know that you got the referral and have made contact with the client.

2. **Do what you say you will when you say you will.** Sadly, I have several business partners who I *know* are trustworthy people of high integrity (this is why I still do business with them), but their actions make me second guess my decision to do business with them. Why? Because they are unreliable.

3. **Be patient and consistent and understand differences.** Trust is a complex blend of emotion or feeling and thoughts. It takes time to develop. Know that some people are overly trusting, to the point of being naïve. Others are not particularly trusting, to the point of being paranoid. If you can figure out someone's style, you can accommodate it. Regardless, being authentic and consistent in your actions will help build trust over time. Evaluate your actions and ask yourself, "Would I trust someone who acts in this way?" The ability to build trust is a skill to learn and practice.

4. **Create a cohesive culture.** If there are others in your business (even if you are a sole proprietor with an assistant who serves as an independent contractor), establish the company culture and sense of mission that you want. Be sure that others know how the work benefits clients, and check out assumptions to be sure you're all on the same page. Doing so is likely to enhance culture, reputation, *and* financial performance.

Staying Focused and Motivated When Results Aren't Immediate

People are not usually ready to take action to hire you or refer to you after one follow-up. In fact, it is likely to take five or ten or more follow-ups before people take action. Think of this like dating: taking action would mean committing to a long-term relationship. While we can certainly all think of exceptions, most couples date for some time before they commit to each another. If it were faster, it would be surprising, but for some reason in business we expect the results to be faster. Maybe because the business courtship period is not quite as fun—it doesn't typically involve candlelight dinners and weekend getaways. If you start to get frustrated that results aren't happening, remind yourself that your goal is to build the foundation of a relationship. At the core of this foundation is trust, as we've just discussed. Reminding yourself that you are building trust that develops over time can keep you focused. That said, there are times when you need to . . .

"Know when to hold 'em and know when to fold 'em"

You may have used all of the ideas we've discussed thus far to initiate and follow up on great relationships, but still nothing is happening. It may be that the person you are trying to initiate a referral relationship or joint venture with is simply not right. Here are three types of people in whom it may be a good idea to stop investing your time and energy:

The "I'm So Swamped" Professional These people are difficult to reach. They are always "swamped" or "under tight deadlines." The challenge with these people is that they are often swamped for good reason—they are in high demand because they are good at what they do. This type of professional might make sense to stay in touch with because when they do things, they are of excellent quality. The challenge is that you don't know exactly when they will be done. You might find a way to work with them on a limited and planned-out basis with clear expectations about time lines and organizational systems.

There is, however, another subtype of this type—those who are all about the drama of being swamped. They create "craziness," and everything is melodramatic when in reality the demands they juggle are similar to what the rest of us juggle. These types can be energy draining, and it is usually wise to limit your involvement with them.

The Nonreciprocator These professionals appreciate your relationship but don't seem to reciprocate. You feel that you do a lot for them but do not receive much in return. Ask yourself if you have been clear about what you'd like and need. Do not expect people to read your mind. Also ask yourself if what you'd like and need is realistic and if they are the people capable of offering those things. Read the next chapter to be sure that what you do to keep in touch with them is perceived as valuable. If not, they are not reciprocating because they do not feel that they have received value. If you are confident that you're providing value and expectations as clearly and consistently as possible, realize that these people might be self-focused and unlikely to reciprocate.

The "Can I Pick Your Brain?" Type These people have not actually paid you for your services. They may think of themselves as friends or colleagues (and you may or may not agree) and feel entitled to ask you for consultation without paying you. They are unlikely to become paid clients or refer paid clients. The challenge occurs when they actually are friends or business associates. I tend to answer questions for nonclients as my time permits, but often I believe that it is unethical for me to provide advice to people who are not clients when I do not know their full situation. I may be tempted to give them some quick advice, but it could do them a disservice when they need something more comprehensive and tailored. In the field of medicine, there is legal precedent for successful lawsuits when physicians give advice to nonpatients. It is generally advisable to keep the brain-picking to a minimum.

Patience is a virtue—sometimes

Are you an impatient person like I am? I'm sometimes surprised that I'm a marketing coach because marketing can be a "slow and steady wins the race" type of field. Our strengths are often our weaknesses and vice versa. I could, for example, see my impatience as a strength because it helps me accomplish a lot quickly and help clients move along quickly as well. The downside, of course, is that I may stop doing something before I see results simply because I've become impatient with it. One solution to this is to look for the little wins along the way and to focus on enjoying and improving the journey rather than simply trying to get to the destination. If you have reason to believe that you're following up in a respectable way, then you may need to just keep going even though you may feel impatient or frustrated at times.

On the flip side, if you are a patient person, you may continue along with something that is unlikely to bring results. You may be unlikely to question why you are not getting results because you don't have a natural sense of urgency. The last thing you want to do is to waste your time and energy, so be sure that you are being patient with activities that are building relationships that will lead to results.

What are these activities that will build relationships that get results? Learn unique ways to stay in touch in the next chapter.

Chapter 7

Give Value—
People Quickly Determine Whether
Something Is Helpful

Try not to become a man of success but a man of value.

—ALBERT EINSTEIN

THERE'S A FASCINATING book called *The Five Love Languages* by Gary Chapman. Chapman says that everyone has a different way of communicating their love, either through

- Words of affirmation
- Quality time
- Gifts
- Acts of service
- Physical touch

Everybody speaks a different language that determines how they express and expect love. Let's say that your significant other is expressive and she feels loved when you tell her how you feel. Her primary love language is words of affirmation. You, on the other hand, like to spend quality time together to show and feel love. You speak the language of quality time. Can you see how easily miscommunication can occur? Couples often get into conflicts and fall out of love with each other because they do not feel loved. You may be speaking a love language but your partner is not hearing it. The solution is to learn what language your partner speaks so you communicate your feelings in his or her language so your feelings get heard.

This is a book on business relationships, not love relationships, so how does all of this apply? It is the same, although the types of languages spoken are different. We need to learn what languages our business partners speak so we can communicate in the ways that are most valuable to them. This goes back to what their goals are and how you can help fill them, as we discussed in the first section.

In my work with clients and my own business partners, I see the five most common languages of love in business as

- **Getting referrals.** These professionals seek to build their businesses, and they love receiving referrals of their ideal clients.
- **Saving time.** These busy professionals value nothing more than time. They likely have several interests outside of work, such as family or sports, and their goal is to be as productive and efficient as possible in their work. They love anything that will save them time—and will love you if you can help them do that!
- **Connecting people.** These people love offering excellent referrals and recommendations to their clients or colleagues. They tend to be well-connected social influencers who appreciate knowing who's the best in their field so they can connect people and resources.
- **Adding intellectual value.** These professionals always want to learn more. They love learning new and interesting things. They seek to maximize the quality of their work and the services they provide.
- **Learning about favorite things.** This language is more personal in nature; it's about stuff they love, any personal thing that you know they are into—dogs, horses, kayaking, traveling, scrapbooking, whatever.

Which languages do you speak? What do you value most right now? Which languages do your referral partners speak? The only way that you can truly add value to your joint venture and referral partners is to understand the language that they speak.

People may have multiple love languages. Your goal is to discover which are the strongest for your referral partners and to customize your keep-in-touch marketing accordingly.

Your clients, unlike potential business partners, typically come to you for a specific service, so it is easier to understand the value that they are looking for. To speak their language is to provide the best possible quality service. Your keep-in-touch marketing will be directly in line with the type of content that they're looking for.

One of my clients, Martina, a physical therapist, served patients with back injuries and had referral relationships with several chiropractors. Together Martina and I determined that her patients' goals were to reduce their pain and increase their mobility. They wanted to feel comfortable with her, and they wanted to be served as efficiently as possible. She spoke their language by providing top-notch services and crystal clear descriptions (including written diagrams) of the exercises they would practice in between sessions. She increased her patients' comfort level by making small talk, showing compassion and empathy, and mirroring their energy and talkativeness. If someone came in and said they were exhausted and spoke little, she helped them relax by remaining on the quieter side rather than peppering them with conversation. Martina met her patients' goals for efficient service by keeping her practice on time unless there was an emergency. The front desk staff let patients know an accurate estimate for when they would be seen so they could do work or make a phone call while they waited if Martina was running behind.

Martina and I discovered that her chiropractor colleagues tended to speak two languages: referrals and time. The five or so chiropractors who referred most to her were relatively recent graduates with young families. They wanted to build their businesses and fill their schedules with referrals and save time so they could be with their children, play sports, and do other things. Martina learned about each of their backgrounds and specialties so she could provide patients who requested referrals for chiropractors with accurate information. She communicated efficiently with these chiropractors by immediately sending over her one-page treatment plan whenever they shared a patient (with the patient's permission, of course, so the professionals could coordinate their care). She left succinct voice mails and included her phone number twice so the chiropractor wouldn't need to listen to the message again if he or she missed a number.

Becoming Fluent and Providing Value

How do we uncover someone's preferred language? It's simple—all you have to do is listen. People usually speak in their preferred language. Going back to love language in intimate relationships—one of my clients, Mario, a busy partner in a law firm, told me that his wife had been feeling stressed out lately. So one night on the way home from work, he stopped to buy her flowers. She was happy with the flowers. Later that evening, however, she said to him, "Honey, I would really feel more supported if you helped out some more. If I encounter one more overflowing trash can or stack of dirty dishes in the sink or trip over one more pair of shoes, I might lose it!" Can you guess what each of their languages are? His is gifts, whereas hers is acts of service. He thought to get her flowers because little gifts cheer him up, but what she really wanted was some help around the house.

One of Mario's goals in our work together to build his practice was to save time. So you can imagine how happy he was to learn that it meant more to his wife for him to spend two minutes taking out the trash than 20 minutes debating what flowers to buy. Simply listen to what people talk about when they get stressed or excited, and you'll soon identify their language. The next step is to practice speaking it.

Giving referrals

If your potential referral partner's language is referrals, begin by getting clear on what types of clients they seek. Learn more about what they specialize in. Familiarize yourself with the types of services they provide by asking for a case study. Understand how what they offer is different from what others in your referral network offer. Of course, you will give referrals only to professionals who you feel can offer excellent services to your clients, friends, family members, or colleagues, so be sure you are knowledgeable and confident about their backgrounds and approaches.

We can be tempted to send people in the direction of someone who we want to get referrals from when that person may or may not be the best match for the particular client. I tend to give clients two to three names of professionals at a time so they can see who best meets their needs rather than to steer them in the direction of one particular person. In doing so, I usually give a quick blurb about each person. You might check out the blurbs that you use with your prospective referrals to be sure that the way that you describe them is accurate. The clients can then decide which professional they have the best chemistry with and whose approach they think will work well for them.

Saving time

If your business partners value saving time and you can find a way to help them do this, they will love you. Sharing resources is an excellent way to do so. For example, you can drop a line to let a business partner know about a new software you've been using that has helped you save time. Or send along articles on a topic that your partner is currently researching. If she lives or works near you and there has been construction and traffic, you can let her know about an alternate route that you discovered—any tips and resources that can save them time will be much appreciated.

Express your respect for their limited time by being as efficient as possible in your communications with them. If you collaborate on a project or client or patient, get them everything they need as quickly as possible. Stick to all of your deadlines.

Connecting people

This is a fun one because you get to play matchmaker for the matchmaker. These professionals have a wide network that they enjoy expanding as a way to build their business and to connect others. Your keep-in-touch action is to introduce them to other people. At the heart of making this one work is an understanding of what each business partner values. Imagine their networks as hot air balloons. The balloons consist of the sundry people in their networks. What brings it all together is their values—the basket. Understand what's in each person's basket. It may be the types of people, such as high-energy people who are out there creating a lot of change in the world. It may be personal values, such as a religious affiliation. It may be the type of work, such as a strong emphasis on research.

Once you understand the types of connections they are attracted to, you can periodically introduce them to others. You can do a three-way e-mail introduction. Or you can send a quick note with a link to the other person's Web site. Or you can send a book or an article by the person and ask your business partner if she'd like you to make the introduction.

Adding intellectual value

Professionals who speak this language love to learn. They have a thirst for knowledge and enjoy learning the latest research. They are likely subscribers of several magazines and newspapers and perhaps listen to National Public Radio. They are especially interested in data and ideas that can help them be better at what they do. Thus, while they are intellectual, they are also practical and want to continuously improve their services. To keep in touch, you can send excellent articles written by other professionals accompanied by a simple message: "I just saw this article and thought you'd find it interesting . . ." You can send journals, magazines, or books. If your referral partner is a business leader, you might drop by her office with a copy of your favorite leadership book. It is ideal to send your own articles from time to time, but it is also nice to send other people's articles. When you send your own, you provide value from the content of the article or book, but you also show your expertise, which increases your credibility and memorability. When you send other people's articles, the effect feels slightly less self-serving, as though you simply saw something and thought it could be beneficial, so you sent it along.

These professionals also love excellent tips that they can pass along to their clients. You can make, for example, a list of "The Top 10 Ways to . . . ," have a brochure-sized pamphlet designed (one page, can be double sided), and have it printed on high-quality paper. Send over a stack of these tip sheets for your business partner to pass along to her clients. If she loves it, give her a list of five or six other tip sheet topics and ask if she'd like more.

Learning about their favorite things

We all have those few things that strike our "I could never talk too much about . . ." buttons. For many of us, it's our kids and pets. It may also be favorite sports teams, activities, geographical locations (such as nearby beaches or mountains), and so on. You should already know some of these things when you use the attention-grabbing and relationship-building tools we discussed in Chapter 2. Stay in touch by asking or sending information about these things. For example, you might drop an e-mail and say, "I remember you saying Joey was into acting, and I noticed that the middle school is putting on a performance of *Charlie & the Chocolate Factory*. Is he in it?" Or you might drop a dog-lover a *New York Times* article about a Labrador who saved someone's life. You may have taken note that your business partner was running in an upcoming marathon and send over a little care package of energy bars and Gatorade for her training. You'll need to keep track of people's interests. One of my clients, a real estate agent in a middle- to upper-class suburb, found that many of her clients had dogs and considered themselves to be "dog people." She created a spreadsheet recording the kinds of dogs that they had.

With these personal things, a little goes a long way. When you have something in common with someone, don't hesitate to share it. For example, if you both have twin boys, send over a photo of your boys playing or being silly with a line like, "Isn't it fun to have twin boys?" Revealing some of yourself builds camaraderie and reinforces the similarities between the two of you. For this to work well, however, you must have made a positive first impression. If they didn't like you, they won't be interested in learning what's new with your twin boys.

Becoming Fluent and Providing Value

ACTION STEPS

1. **Create a specific spreadsheet for referrals.** In order to best make referrals, create a spreadsheet with the following categories:

Name

Address

Phone number

E-mail

Preferred way for new clients to contact

Specialty

Description of ideal clients

Office hours (Do they do evenings, weekends?)

Style of work (In-person, telephone, Skype, hourly, monthly programs?)

Other factors of interest (If it's a medical field, do they take insurance?)

2. **Keep a live list of your favorite time-savers.** Add to this list any time you discover something new that you can pass along to others. Focus on finding things that are free so you don't always pass along paid resources. Ask others about their favorite ways to save time in different areas of life and work, and add these ideas to your list.

3. **Connect different people at least twice a month.** Get in the habit of making connections by beginning with your current database and looking for great connections. (Don't connect the same people more often than once every month or two, though, or they'll wonder why you're suddenly so interested in connecting them with everyone.) Once you've had some experience connecting people, you won't need to look for connections any more; they will just be apparent to you.

4. **Set up Google Alerts for your connection's name.** You'll get an alert sent to you by e-mail whenever your connection's name appears somewhere new online. You can then send a card to congratulate her for an award she received or e-mail her to let her know how much you enjoyed her article. You can "Like" her new content on Facebook or retweet her tweets.

5. **Set up Google Alerts for your connection's intellectual interests.** For example, if your connection is an organizational psychologist, you can set up an alert for "emotional intelligence" and send along interesting articles you find.

6. **Set up Google Alerts for your connection's personal interests.** For example, if your connection is a cycling enthusiast, you can send along links to great articles on the best places to ride bikes in your area and so on.

Generating Automated Content

The ideas above will be, for the most part, personal and customized in nature. If you have 100 important connections, you can't rely on those strategies alone for your monthly contacts, or you would be doing nothing else. Ideally, plan to keep in touch with people one to four times per month (or more if that is typical in your industry). Every couple of months, incorporate one of the love language ways to add value discussed above. For the rest of the times, you'll need to use social networking, your blog, e-mail marketing, or other automated strategies to keep in touch. I think the best keep-in-touch marketing systems use a combination of electronic and physical methods. Most people have a newsletter, but this is not enough. I've gotten my best results when I've combined my newsletter with other methods, such as sending out cards, videos, and other things.

You'll balance the more time-consuming personal keep-in-touch marketing with excellent automated content that goes out to everyone in the same way at the same time. We are all inundated with e-mails and other ways in which content comes to us. So the challenge in marketing with content these days is to come up with unique, high-caliber content. And we are all strapped for time and can't spend half our week researching and writing articles, so the second challenge becomes creating content quickly. Let's look at some strategies to create unique and quick content now.

Create unique content

People get hundreds of e-mails each day. Why should they read yours? Because you offer such unique, valuable, and compelling information that they can't help themselves no matter how busy they are. You want to feel great about the content you put out there and be assured that people really benefit from it. You want it to stand out and for people to not hit the delete key when they see your message.

My favorite resource for generating unique content is a book by Mark Levy, *Accidental Genius: Using Writing to Generate Your Best Ideas, Insight, and Content.* In it he describes the process of freewriting. Freewriting, he explains, is a way to access your inner creativity and genius without your internal editor getting in the way. Typically, when our minds enter new territory, the internal editor jumps in and shuts things down. New thoughts requires work, and our bodies are designed to keep things the same (principle of homeostasis), so it can be difficult to go in different directions. The unfortunate result is we tend to rehash ideas we've had or heard before. Freewriting is a fast, uncensored process of taking your mind into new territories and coming up with fresh, innovative ideas and content. In *Accidental Genius*, Levy shares 15 powerful ways to use freewriting. Here are a couple of my favorites:

1. **Use prompts to get your writing going.** Prompts are open-ended beginnings. Give yourself 10 minutes to write; get started with the prompt, but feel free to go wherever the writing takes you. Don't be roped in by the prompt. Freewriting is often a circuitous journey. Examples of prompts include:
   - I'd love to learn about . . .
   - My favorite thing about this cold weather is . . .
   - If I knew I'd be successful I'd . . .
2. **Don't come up with an idea—come up with a hundred.** It's actually much more difficult to come up with one good idea than it is to come up with dozens of ideas. One idea leads to the next one, which leads to the next, and your great idea (or many great ideas) will probably be in there. It's actually much faster and more fun this way.

3. **Open up words.** This creative technique Levy devised allows you to imbue personal meaning into a word that may be contrite, cliché, overused, unclear, or unspecific. The process includes four steps. First, choose a word that you want to open up. Second, write a common definition for the word. Third, write about whether you agree or disagree with this word and your reasons for doing so. Fourth, write a paragraph about your new understanding of that word.

Sandra, a life coach, wanted to be sure that her content helped her to build her credibility. She was concerned that "life coaching" had a negative connotation for some of her corporate clients, so she used Open Up Words to explore the meaning and came up with a couple of great, personal stories about her journey into life coaching and the unique approach she took. Inspired by this approach, she generated 100 article ideas, 20 of which she developed into short articles. Over the course of a few days, she created an entire year's worth of compelling content for her e-zine (electronic newsletter). She told me that several of her new clients hired her because of the unique ideas she shared in these articles.

Create quick content

Let's be practical. You simply don't have dozens of hours each month to create content to send out to keep in touch with your prospects. And even if you did, some of that time might be better used by meeting with people in person—or taking a day off and going to the park. Here are five ways to create great content quickly and easily:

1. **Create one long piece and edit it.** Coming up with the topic and getting going is often the hardest part of creating content. Once you get going, you may have a lot to say on the topic. So spend a couple of hours creating a video or extended article. Then edit it into three to five short pieces. This process works especially well if you do something like "3 Steps to . . ." or "The 5 Little Known Ways to . . ." so each segment has a logical beginning and conclusion. It is also great if each piece can stand

alone in case someone misses one. If you send your content out by e-mail, include a link to previous related pieces, and at the end, offer all of them together. I like using three to five pieces per topic because it feels easy and manageable (no one wants to learn 28 steps that they need to take), but you can go up to ten.

2. **Let other people create content.** The downside to sharing other people's content is that those in your audience will not learn more about your ideas and approach as well as if the content were your own. Manage this downside by including a discussion at the end that includes your ideas or by selecting people who offer ideas that are complimentary to your own. For example, I work with small business owners and service professionals on marketing their businesses, but I do not specialize in things like organization or accounting that they and their businesses can certainly benefit from, so I frequently have guest bloggers share ideas on my blog. Don't use other people's content as your primary strategy. Use something like 80 percent of your own content and 20 percent of other people's.

3. **Cocreate content.** An easy way to do this is by interviewing people who have great ideas that synergize with your own. Look for people who will graciously share content without being overly promotional. Offer to act as a reporter, someone who will promote their books or services for them so they don't have to. This usually helps people to deliver better content and not have to worry about promoting themselves, and it gives a higher quality feel to the interview. You can do interviews by audio or video. You can have them transcribed for more free content or to create a paid information product.

4. **Create a Top 10 list.** This is different from the first technique because it is one succinct list that will go out all at once. For example, a financial planner may offer "The Top 10 Things You Can Do to Save for Your Child's College," or a fitness trainer can provide "The Top 10 Mistakes Most People Make When Doing Crunches." Include tips as short bolded sentences or phrases, and include a sentence or two describing each tip. You can probably

sit down and create ten Top 10 lists in an hour. Just don't send them all out back to back. People can't resist reading Top 10 lists because of the curiosity factor—we want to know the best things we could do or the worst things we should be avoiding.

5. **Take a writing retreat.** The amount of time and energy it takes to sit down and start writing in small intervals is significant. Save all of this time and energy by doing it at once. Take one day every couple of months and spend it writing. Begin your writing day by using a freewriting exercise, such as one of those described above. Maybe you could use a prompt like "My clients value . . ." or "People want to learn about . . ." or "I want to share . . ."

Make sure that your e-mails get read

Now that you've created all of this excellent automated content, we need to be sure that your e-mails get read. The first step is to do your best to ensure that your e-mails don't end up in spam filters. Do this by using e-mail distribution services (rather than pasting dozens of e-mail addresses into the blind carbon copy field of your message) that have high deliverability rates. These change often, but at the time of this writing, some of the top ones include AWeber, MailChimp, iContact, and Constant Contact. Avoid including words in your subject lines that are likely to trigger spam filters (such as *free*). Be sure that you do not send spam by using opt-in only. This means that you cannot add someone's e-mail to your list unless you have their permission to do so. There was a recent debate on a discussion list that I'm on about whether it's okay to add someone to your e-mail list if you've exchanged business cards. I do not think that this is okay. You can, however, e-mail the person and include a link for a free giveaway and sign-up for your newsletter. You can also pass around sign-up sheets for people to add their names and e-mail addresses if they'd like your free giveaway.

The second thing to do is to ensure that people open your message when it arrives in their inbox. The most important consideration here is the e-mail subject line. The goal of the subject line is to get people to open the message, so the most important task is to arouse curiosity. Here are my favorite tips on creating compelling subject lines:

- **Ask a question.** It is hard for us to read a question and not try to think of (and want to know) the answer. Questions stimulate curiosity, which increases your open-rate.
- **Use incomplete sentences . . .** The ellipsis (three periods in a row) is powerful in the same way that a question is. People don't like to be left hanging and are curious to find out more.
- **Include numbers.** Subject lines such as "The top 3 ways to jump start your weight loss plan" are compelling because, again, the mind does not like ambiguity and uncertainty. We can't help but wonder what these three ways are. If the subject line were "Great ways to jump-start your weight loss plan," it would be less compelling.
- **Be specific.** People need to know exactly what they are getting if they invest their valuable time in reading your e-mail. Something like, "Molly McCune's Monthly E-zine" or "News from The Wellness Spa" is not going to cut it. If you want to include the name of your e-zine, do so in brackets, but include the topic of interest in that particular edition next to the name of the e-zine.
- **Offer something unexpected.** When something is a little bit puzzling or confusing, it stands out and makes us curious to learn more. An Internet marketer and best-selling author recently sent out an e-mail with the subject line "The Slacker's Approach to Success." We typically associate success with hard work, so this subject line is unexpected and powerful.

The third thing to do is to make sure that your e-mails pass the first impression test. If people see huge blocks of text, they will feel that it is too much work to wade through it. Plus people typically scan messages. So shorten paragraphs, and include bullets, boldface, and numbers to break up the text.

Becoming Fluent and Providing Value

ACTION STEPS

1. **Do three 10-minute freewrites.** Write quickly and without censor to open up your mind and generate unique and creative content. Write about whatever comes to mind, or use prompts or tools such as the ones previously described. You might not create usable content from these three freewriting sessions alone, but you'll gain comfort with the process and can use it to move your thinking forward and create content in the future.

2. **Break up your articles.** Go through some of your longer articles and break them up into two or three parts to extend your keep-in-touch. Remember that less is typically more with e-mail marketing. Receiving a verbose article or e-zine is overwhelming to a lot of people.

3. **Post articles on your blog but not in your e-zine.** I often do this to keep my e-zine from getting long and intimidating. I include some personal stories, tips, and news in the e-zine and a link to read the article on the blog. Bringing people onto your blog is nice because they can comment there and you can further build your relationships rather than simply deliver one-way communication.

4. **Frame outreach marketing on recent results.** Often when we receive a piece of marketing from someone, we assume that they're doing it because they need more business. To counteract this, be in touch with people regularly as we've discussed, and include positive results in your marketing. For example, a real estate agent can send out a postcard that says, "In the past three months, I've sold these homes in your neighborhood . . ." This focuses on the use of data and the similarity principle discussed earlier since people share a common situation (neighborhood) with their neighbors.

5. **Brainstorm 20 subject lines for each e-mail.** We usually start to sound more natural and create more interesting ideas when we stop trying to come up with one and start brainstorming a whole bunch.

6. **Look at your message for one second.** How do you feel? Be honest. If you feel that it is a lot of work to read all the information, others will feel the same way. Break it up. Include white space, images, and graphics to add visual appeal.

Now that you have some ideas about how to create great quality content, let's consider how to get people active around your content and stimulate discussions.

Chapter 8

Stimulate Discussion— People Become Invested When They're Involved

---

Nothing great was ever achieved without enthusiasm.

—RALPH WALDO EMERSON

CAN YOU FIGURE out the difference between these two scenarios?

- **Scenario 1.** You update your status on Facebook: "Just finished a delicious dinner at a new Japanese restaurant around the corner from my house. What a treat to go out in the middle of the week and enjoy great food and conversation. Sushi is my favorite." You check back a couple hours later and no one has commented or "Liked" your post. The next morning, you check back into Facebook and only one person has commented on your post— your mom. "Strange," you think to yourself, feeling a little disappointed. "I'm sure that other people like sushi and don't get to go out midweek very much. I'm surprised that no one else commented."

- **Scenario 2.** You update your status on Facebook: "Sushi and sake tonight! Anyone else a fan?" You check back a couple hours later and have several Likes and a few comments such as, "I could go for some California rolls right now," and "Have you tried the new place on Front Street? It's awesome!" and "Have a shot of sake for me." You're happy to have stimulated some discussion, and you got a couple great restaurant recommendations.

You probably have some ideas about why the second was more effective. Let's explore the reasons.

To get discussion going in social media or other places, think of the acronym EARS, like you want people to listen with all ears. Your conversation must be:

- **Engaging.** This means that people feel that you're speaking directly to or with them, not at them. You want your posts to sound conversational and not like entries out of your daily planner or journal.
- **Affective.** Affect is another word for emotion. Affective communication has energy and emotion to it.
- **Relatable.** We become engaged when we can relate to something on a personal level. This means that we've experienced or thought something similar before.
- **Simple.** Remember that our brains and bodies are designed to conserve energy, so if something is too complicated, we resist it. To be simple, a message should have one meaning and should be as brief as possible to convey that meaning.

Let's consider some ways to include EARS in your marketing, particularly in speaking and in social media since those are two areas where discussion is essential.

Engaging Is Everything

Have you ever heard someone speak and felt that the speaker was truly charismatic? If so, the speaker was engaging. The ability to engage others is the hallmark of charisma. You don't have to be super-outgoing or funny to be charismatic. Some of the most effective and charismatic speakers I have seen actually have more of a calm, captivating presence about them. You cannot be effective or charismatic without being engaging and being able to hold people's interest.

Attract and hold attention with strong visuals

Engaging is closely linked to attraction. We are drawn to certain things more than others. One of the most powerful of these things is visual imagery. Of course you should look your best, but there are other ways to include visual imagery to engage people:

- **Include strong imagery in your PowerPoint presentations.** Pictures draw us in. I particularly like to use photography because it is instantly recognizable to the eye. Unlike clip art, which can feel dated and amateurish, a clear, crisp photograph tends to feel modern and sophisticated.
- **Use minimal words in your PowerPoint presentations.** Rely instead on imagery to guide your discussion. I attended a presentation by Seth Godin, and his slides consisted of only one image or a couple of words per slide. This is a very effective way to engage your audience. When there are a lot of words on your slides, people read. Reading is passive. When, on the other hand, there are a few words or images, people listen. Listening (which is different from hearing) is active.
- **Use imagery in social media.** I've noticed that in general, the status updates on my page Facebook.com/MarketingPsych that include visual imagery get a significantly greater number of Likes and comments than those that do not. Do not, however, use images in all status updates because the variety is

compelling. It is okay and in fact a good idea to use imagery in all of your blog posts. Including an image in the same location of each post unifies your blog and provides a sense of calm and consistency. You can now include images on Twitter or use TwitPic.

- **Create videos.** When I first returned to work after maternity leave with my second son, I did a webinar on the psychology of influence for a group of mortgage brokers. I had the option of including live video of myself in the presentation. I was torn because I know how much more engaging it is to include video, but after two months of sleep deprivation, let's just say I had a face for radio. (I did do the video and was thankful for makeup.) Videos are one of the most engaging types of marketing because not only are they visual, but they also include movement and sound, which capture attention. Aim for balance in your sound and movement. Too much movement and nonstop talking is disconcerting and causes us to disengage and pay attention to something more stimulating. Too little movement and monotonous sound is dull, and so we disengage and pay attention to something less stimulating.

- **Consider your surroundings.** If you're hosting a workshop, for example, find a setting that provides the energy you want people to feel (serene, upbeat, inspired, etc.). Again, we need to find the right balance here. If the environment is too sterile in feel, people can translate that feeling onto you and become less engaged. If the environment is too complex, people can feel overwhelmed, so they tune out rather than pay attention to you. When newborn babies sense too much stimulation in the environment, their neurological systems shut down so they don't go into overdrive (this is one reason that babies tend to fall asleep at parties and restaurants). This reaction is not as strong in adults, but it is still present.

- **Strategically use color.** Think about your audience and what is attractive to them. Entrepreneur coach Ali Brown currently has a great photo on her Facebook page with a bright pink background. That photo is engaging.

Captivate with questions

In addition to the tools above that use visuals to engage people, my next favorite strategy is to use questions. In the last chapter, we discussed how questions can be excellent subject lines for e-mails because people will open your e-mail in search of the answers. Some other great ways to ask questions are:

- In your tweets or status updates in social media.
- In the titles of your articles and blog posts.
- In your presentations. Even if you are delivering a lecture that is not designed to be interactive, ask rhetorical questions. These questions transition people from passively hearing to listening and thinking, which make them engaged.
- In your print marketing. If you have a two-sided postcard, you might include a question on one side (just know that you can't be sure which side someone will see first).

The key to effective use of questions is that they get people thinking but do not require a ton of work. The way to do this is by being as specific as possible. Especially in social media, people want to be efficient and move on. They don't want to sit around pondering your question. Unless your audience is unique in some way, if you post "What's the meaning of life?" you are unlikely to get a lot of responses. If, however, you post, "What was something meaningful you did today?" you're likely to get responses.

Engaging Is Everything

ACTION STEPS

1. **Begin your photo database.** You can include pictures that you have taken, pictures of you, and pictures that friends and family have taken— as long as they are well-lit and in focus. Sometimes the "autocorrect" features of simple photo-editing software is all that you need to enhance

the lighting and colors of your photos. You can find excellent, low-cost stock photos online at sites like istockphoto.com. You can find great free photos at sites like sxc.hu or wylio.com. Just read the usage agreements because some require that you notify the photographers when you use their photos.

2. **Revise your slides.** Go through your PowerPoint presentations and challenge yourself to use five or fewer words per slide. Use some slides that include only one photo to emphasize key points and add visual interest.

3. **Film yourself for fun and learning.** If you are new to creating videos, do not try to create a finished product the first time you're in front of the camera. It takes some time and experience to gain comfort. Remember that people respond more to nonverbal than verbal communication, so your body language is very important. Watch the videos as a learning tool. Don't criticize yourself—you will look much worse to yourself than to other people. Instead, look for a couple objective things to practice, such as using your hands to gesture a bit more if you are still as a rock or using your hands a bit less if you look like you're conducting an orchestra. Strike a balance between being a motionless talking head and a nonstop moving bobble head. Speak to the camera in one position for 30 seconds, then move slightly (such as with a tilt of the head), then move largely after a minute or two (such as with a weight shift or change in the placement of your hands).

4. **Speak from notes but don't read scripts.** When you speak before an audience or on video, you don't want to have to completely rely on your memory. That can be stressful and can put you more into your head, which breaks your connection with your audience because you're thinking about what will come next. Use brief notes or slides to guide you. You also don't want to read from a script because you will be connecting with a piece of paper rather than your audience. Get more speaking tips in my book *The Confident Speaker*, which I wrote with executive speech coach Harrison Monarth.

5. **Skype when possible.** Suggest Skyping rather than meeting with people by phone. Seeing each other will enhance connection and engagement.

6. **Edit your questions.** Go through questions that you ask in a presentation or in social media and revise them to be as specific as possible. For example, if you were going to ask, "What motivates you to keep your home and office organized?" instead ask, "At the end of a long day, what can you think about to help you put the dishes in the sink rather than let them pile up on the counter?" People pass over broad questions and think about answers to specific questions.

7. **When speaking, pause after asking a question.** If you ask a rhetorical question that you want your audience to think about, pause for a moment before moving on. Without this pause, the question-asking technique can backfire because your audience will be thinking about your question as you speak rather than listening to you. Pausing also breaks up the monotony of a presentation and keeps people engaged.

Be Affective to Be Effective

The Facebook post in scenario 1 at the beginning of this chapter was not affective. It did not contain emotion. To connect with people, you don't want to be like a news reporter delivering news in a detached and professional manner. If you do this, people feel that you do not care, and, therefore, why should they?

Emotions are contagious. In psychology, we call this "emotional contagion." Researchers have found that viewing positive emotions in someone leads to positive emotions in ourselves. Emotional contagion can be especially strong if the person expressing the emotion is charismatic or is in a leadership position. The authors of *Primal Leadership*, Daniel Goleman, Richard Boyatzis, and Annie McKee, describe how leaders' emotions resonate with others. We have mirror neurons in our brains that reflect the emotions of others, and we are particularly likely to be influenced by people in a leadership role.

Emotional contagion can be a subconscious or a conscious process. Subconscious emotional contagion is thought to exist when someone displays an emotion and we unconsciously imitate the display of emotion (e.g., smile). As a result of our behavior (smile), our emotions shift and we experience an emotion similar to that of the sender. In this type of emotional contagion, greater displays of emotion can lead to greater feelings of emotion. A barely visible smile is less likely to be mimicked by someone and therefore less likely to create an emotional change, whereas a broad teeth-baring grin is likely to have a more substantial effect.

Conscious emotional contagion is thought to result from ambiguous social situations. When we're in an unfamiliar or otherwise uncertain situation, we tend to look around at other people to match their emotions. In this type of emotional contagion, greater displays of emotion do not necessarily lead to greater feelings of emotion; rather, people are influenced by their perceptions of the authenticity of the emotion. Let's say that you meet with a new client for the first time. In an attempt to make the client feel comfortable, you flash a big smile. You, however, are nervous about the meeting, and your nerves have the better of you, so while you show a smile, it does not feel genuine. Your client is less likely to have a positive emotional contagion experience.

An interesting 2006 study published in the *Journal of Marketing* investigated just how "service with a smile" works. Two hundred and twenty-three undergraduate students were told that the researchers were testing a new movie consulting service. The student would be a customer and meet one on one with a consultant. The consultants were actually trained actors, some of whom engaged in "surface acting" and provided service with a smile. Surface acting is consistent with the subconscious emotional contagion theories. Other "consultants" engaged in "deep acting," a type of method acting where the actors truly experience the emotion they portray. Deep acting is consistent with the conscious emotional contagion theories. The researchers thought that both types of service with a smile (whether the smile was the result of surface or deep acting) would enhance customer emotions, satisfaction, and loyalty. They were surprised to discover that only the second type of service (deep acting) enhanced these factors. The authenticity but not the frequency of smiling made the difference. Unlike prior research, mimicry effects (from surface acting) did not occur. The authors postulate that mimicry effects may occur in short periods of time but fade during a more extensive service interaction. The more important factor is the authenticity of the service provider's emotions.

What makes an emotion be perceived as authentic? One of the things that people look for is a genuine smile, also known as the Duchenne smile, after the physician Guillaume Duchenne, who discovered the two different types of smiles. In the mid 1800s, he was researching facial expressions and discovered that all smiles involved the zygomatic major muscles around the mouth. Only one type of smile (the Duchenne smile) involved the orbicularis oculi muscles. These muscles create creases around our eyes (crow's feet). The Duchenne smile is perceived as more genuine. It is hard to fake because the small orbicularis oculi muscles are difficult to control voluntarily.

The most reliable way, therefore, to give a Duchenne smile is to actually *be* happy. How can you just be happy, especially when faced with a challenging client or customer? Well, the first and most obvious thing you can do is to truly be happy with your work. Focus on working only with the clients that energize and inspire you. Start saying no to referrals of your non-ideal clients. Charge what you are worth so you don't have to overwork. Outsource the parts of your work that don't utilize your natural strengths and talents so you can focus on what you do best.

The next thing you can do is to act. You can't always be in a good mood, so on the days that you are not, learn to change your mood through acting. As we discussed above, there are two types of acting: surface acting and deep acting. We learned that when service professionals engage in deep acting, customers have a more pleasant experience. But isn't acting exhausting and insincere? Alicia Grandey of The Pennsylvania State University set out to answer this question. She sent surveys to administrative assistants in a large Midwestern university and received 131 responses. She chose to focus on administrative assistants because of the high emotional demands of their jobs—they are expected to be continuously pleasant and courteous. Coworkers of the administrative assistants completed a questionnaire about the assistants' interactions with the public. The results were interesting: Deep acting had a positive impact on interactions with the public and was not found to be emotionally exhausting; surface acting, on the other had, did *not* have positive impact and *was* found to be emotionally exhausting. Implications of these findings are that we may actually do well to engage in deep acting because of the positive cycle of feelings that results: the customer feels more positive, you feel more positive, and so on.

So how do you do deep acting and shift your emotions? One way is to use empathy. If you are faced with an irritated customer, remind yourself that she may have stressful things going on in her life and that she doesn't mean to be rude to you. When we get into a place of acceptance rather than judgment (of ourselves or anyone else), we let go of negative emotions. The more that you know about your clientele, the more you can ask yourself what may be going through their minds. You can also ask them. One of my clients, Jordan, a real estate agent, found himself faced with a frustrated client. "Why isn't my house selling?" the client demanded. Jordan felt an initial pang of anxiety but remained positive by reminding himself about the stress his client was under because he had already purchased another home. Jordan was able to remain positive and provide a warm, reassuring smile and response to his client.

Be Affective to Be Effective

ACTION STEPS

1. **Practice improving your mood to improve your bottom line.** Your positive mood leads to a positive mood in your client, which increases rapport, satisfaction, and loyalty. Mood and behavior are directly linked—you can shift your mood by changing your behavior. Increase mood-enhancing behaviors such as exercise and enjoyable recreation. Decrease stress-inducing behaviors such as procrastination and rushing.

2. **Hire people who make you feel good.** When you interview people, pay attention to your sense of the authenticity of their smiles—your clients and customers will feel the same. Recognize that people may be anxious during an interview. Anxiety usually subsides over time, so pay closer attention to their affect (expression of emotion) at the end of the interview because that is likely to be more representative of how they would behave outside of an interview.

3. **Hire well-qualified people and provide regular trainings.** If people are not qualified or are not given the ongoing support they need, they

are likely to feel stressed, which can negatively affect both them and your clients.

4. **Help frontline staff learn deep acting skills.** Remember that deep acting isn't acting so much as learning to shift one's emotions. A method acting coach or psychologist can help people learn how to change their emotions.

5. **Learn and teach empathy.** If you find yourself jumping into a negative mind-set, take a step back and ask yourself what may be going on to affect the person you're speaking with. Maybe he's nervous or tired or stressed. When you don't take it personally, you can remain positive. If you have frontline staff, teach them this skill as well.

If You Aren't Relatable, You're Invisible

In order for people to participate, they need to feel comfortable. If someone feels insecure, intimidated, or otherwise bad while around you, he will not join you in the discussions you lead. People know that as your audience, the more engaged they are, the more they support you. When audience members answer your questions or people join your LinkedIn group, they know that they are supporting you. They choose to do so for the benefit they will receive. But they will not want to join you—and support you—if they do not see you as relatable and likeable.

Be the best you can be—but don't be perfect

Remember how we like people who are like us? This is the law of similarity. Do you think you're perfect? Probably not. In fact, we are our own worst critics. Because we don't see ourselves as perfect, we don't relate to people who come across as too perfect.

We also like to interact with people who make us feel good about ourselves. Have you ever been around someone who is a little too perfect—too smart, too skinny, too attractive? How do you feel about yourself after this interaction? According to the law of social comparison, we naturally compare ourselves with others who are similar to us to see how we measure up. We often like to be around someone who is a little "better" than we see ourselves, but if we see someone as way "better," we feel intimidated and feel worse about ourselves. As a result, we shut down and shy away—things that do not stimulate interaction and discussion.

Earlier, I've recommended that you be attractive to get attention, be a charismatic storyteller to engage emotion, and be smart to be credible. And now I'm telling you not to be perfect. What gives? Well first, don't be too much of any of these things. You don't want to come across as a know-it-all supermodel.

Second, balance out your great qualities with display of your foibles, quirks, and insecurities. I have a theory that one of the reasons that celeb-reality television is so popular is that we like to see celebrities as people like ourselves. We like to see their everyday struggles and know that while they may have perfect hair, clothes, makeup, cars, and houses, they are not different from us, and in fact there is typically a downside to the seemingly perfect life. Share some of your faux pas and social gaffes. Share your hard times and challenging experiences; remember that we can't help but root for the underdog. In social media, I often share silly mistakes I made (I certainly have a nice arsenal to choose from) and my weaknesses (with chocolate typically leading the pack).

Be professional while being human

A closely related topic to being too perfect is being too professional. One of my clients, Anne, a self-help author and motivational speaker, was getting ready to deliver a keynote address. As she rehearsed with me, I did not feel engaged or inspired. She was paying me and I found myself getting distracted, so as an audience member I don't know how invested I would have been in her talk.

At the end, I gave her feedback. I asked her how she wanted to come across to her audience. "Professional," she told me.

"Would you rather be professional or relatable?" I asked.

"Well, both," Anne responded.

"Think of the last talk you attended. As you sat in the audience, would you have preferred that the speaker was professional or relatable?"

"Oh, definitely relatable," she said.

Our focus on ourselves kills us. We think about our own needs and not our audience. We make assumptions about what they want, but really those assumptions are based on our own wants, needs, and insecurities.

Anne is a lovely person who had great value to share with her audience. She was not an egomaniac who had a strong need to be seen as an authority and thus needed to be seen as "professional." Quite the contrary—in reality, she was nervous about coming across as not confident, qualified, or expert in her field (even though she was) so she tried a little too hard to be professional.

"Anne," I suggested, "I want you to think of a time when you struggled with this topic that you're offering advice about."

"Okay . . ." she responded, tentative.

"I want you to tell that story."

"Won't that make me lose credibility with the audience?"

"It can have the opposite effect because it can help people relate to you and your topic," I said. "Try it."

Needless to say, Anne did try it and her story was a hit. People were involved throughout her talk. They sat forward in their chairs; they made eye contact with her. They smiled and laughed and nodded. Afterwards, many audience members came up to speak with her. She told me that it was the best response she had received from a talk to date. Remember that people listen to the radio station WiiFM—"What's in it for me?" If they can't quickly tell what's in it for them, they will tune out. The more relatable you are, the more they'll see what's in it for them.

If you have an inclination toward comedy, a little self-deprecating humor can also go a long way. Remember that you are looking to strike the balance between being the credible expert on your topic and being a relatable human being. Comics need to be 100 percent relatable so they can use as much self-deprecating humor as they like. Experts need to be seen as authorities as well, so throw in some self-deprecating humor if you like, but keep it to a minimum, with maybe a few jokes in a 45-minute presentation. A little joking will enhance the perception of your confidence (we need to be confident to make fun of ourselves), but a lot will undermine the perception of your confidence (if we put ourselves down every other sentence, we will seem insecure).

Be universally relatable

There are some things that people can relate to universally. Certain facial expressions (such as the Duchenne smile) are experienced the same way across cultures. Sunshine tends to make people feel good. Salespeople who smile more and are optimistic (your mind-set gets reflected in your behavior) tend to be more successful.

Incorporate relatable topics into your communications on two levels: First, incorporate things that are relatable on a human level. This builds a sense of human connection, understanding, and trust and serves as a foundation for relationships. Second, incorporate things that are particularly relatable to your audience. This builds your credibility, provides value, and enhances business relationships. Let's say that you own a business that provides food, laundry, and cleaning services to families with young children. Your primary audience is new mothers, and you're a new mom yourself. You could open up great discussions with your audience such as:

Universal Level
- **Blog post title.** "How I Created 10 Extra Minutes in My Day"
- **Tweet.** Breakthrough ways to be more healthy and happy in this article . . .
- **Facebook status update.** Didn't get my morning cup of coffee today. Will I survive until lunch?

Audience Level
- **Blog post title.** "When a 10-Minute Shower Feels Like a Caribbean Getaway"
- **Tweet.** Wow the kids are napping at the same time! There's so much to do, someone will surely be up by the time I decide.
- **Facebook status update.** What dinner has just 5 ingredients and 3 servings of veggies that kids will love? Find out on my blog . . .

Another common but very effective way to provide universally relatable material is by using quotes. When I began my Facebook page, my online business manager, Raven Howard, helped me create a quote contest. Hundreds of people posted quotes on the wall. At the end, we sent out a link to download a PDF with all of the quotes. Even though we've all heard and seen quotes a million times, we can't help but to like them. Good quotes are relatable and inspiring. They are a great way to share a deep concept succinctly, and are often retweeted on Twitter. Just don't overdo your use of quotes because it's more important to share your original ideas. Quotes can be a great way to begin a presentation, blog post, or article (or chapter, as you see in this book and many others), because they tend to be relatable and put people into an open, curious, and inspired mind-set.

If You Aren't Relatable, You're Invisible

ACTION STEPS

1. **Be honest: Do you tend to under-share or over-share personal information?** If you tend to be on the reserved side and maintain strict privacy, try sharing a bit more of your personality. If you tend to be an open book who gives TMI (too much information), scale it back a bit.

2. **Write a list of things you have in common with your audience.** You may do several lists for different types of audiences, business partners, and clients. Use this list to guide stories and tidbits that you share.

3. **Do the "Can you relate?" test.** You probably don't want to say or write this out loud, but it can be a nice way to screen your stories and social media posts. If you're about to post a little story about your dog ("My dog Maggie just jumped up and ate my food off the counter for the second time today!"), can you relate? This is a Tweet I sent out. It passed the "Can you relate?" test since much of my audience includes dog owners.

4. **Make a list of great quotes.** This list will come in handy when you haven't posted in social media in a while but don't have a current update to use. I highlight quotes in yellow once I've used them so I don't use them again.

Simple Is Superior

It is often tempting to go the complex route. Complex can be seen as more intelligent, interesting, or thought-provoking. We mistakenly assume that people will follow us just because we get what we're saying. This is the "fish in water" problem. The complexity of an ocean is familiar to fish, and they don't know any different. A fish may be able to communicate well with another fish in the ocean. But what if the fish needed to communicate with a turtle or a seagull? Or a fish in a lake or pond or fishbowl? Just because something is familiar or simple to you does not mean that it will be to others.

Know your audience

There is a time and a place for complexity of information. In general, complex does not engender discussion. Let's say that you give a presentation, and in one segment, you list 10 important pieces of information. You feel good that you're showing great detail and highlighting your specialized skill set. As an audience member, I'm sitting there trying to process all 10 pieces of information that you just listed. I want to ask a question, but by the time I organize my thoughts, the moment has passed and you're on to something else. This does not promote discussion. The general rule of thumb is: the broader your audience, the less detail to include. If your presentation was on an area in which I was also an expert, I could easily process your 10 pieces of information. Greater levels of detail and specificity can make audiences more involved if they are also experts in your topic.

You don't have to say it all up front

I often write an e-mail and then edit it down by 50 percent or more. It is more difficult to write something concise than something wordy. It may take a little more time to craft a message that delivers all of the crucial information in a pithy manner, but it is worth it. Ironically, when you quickly give someone what they need, they are likely to take more time to have a discussion with you.

Imagine that someone calls you with an idea for a joint venture. He takes several minutes with a spiel about his background, idea, and so on. As he talks, you begin to feel anxious that this conversation will take a long time, and you start feeling uncomfortable as you think of the things that you're being pulled away from. You aren't really listening, and the caller is not creating the positive emotional responses that we know are so important. You make an excuse about why you have to go, and the caller has not successfully initiated a new relationship. Imagine a different scenario: Someone calls you. He introduces himself in a sentence and shares his idea for a joint venture in another sentence. Then he switches gears and discusses why he is interested in you (this hits on several of the key things we've discussed, such as capturing attention by showing your interest in the other person and highlighting what's in it for them). In just a handful of sentences in under a minute, the caller has engaged you, and you will likely be engrossed in a back-and-forth discussion.

Let's say that you see that one of your connections just posted a status update on Facebook so you send her an instant message (chat) through Facebook. Keep it simple—something like "Really enjoyed your update about the snowstorm, thanks for sharing!" And be sure to comment or Like it on their page as well. This simple message is likely to get a response that may or may not lead to more extensive discussion. If it doesn't, that is fine; you have still furthered the potential for a relationship. And if it does, great, you have moved the relationship along.

It is a common misconception that we need to say everything right away because it is likely to be our only shot. Instead, the more likely scenario is that if you say everything right away, it will be your only shot because the person will be done with the conversation. Good conversations are like a tennis game. The ball goes back and forth. It is up to both people to continue the conversation. Don't feel that you need to do all the work, and don't feel that you need to get it all in at the beginning.

Simplify with schemas

In psychology and cognitive neuroscience, schemas are mental maps or ways of viewing the world. Our schemas can help us to simplify complex concepts by fitting them into our existing frameworks. It is like filing papers into folders (schemas) and placing them in your filing cabinet (your memory). Schemas can be helpful or harmful. Dr. Jeffrey Young has developed an empirically validated process called schema therapy that helps people to identify and modify unhelpful mental schemas. Someone who has many difficult childhood experiences of people dying or leaving them may develop a schema such as "People abandon me," which creates fear, anxiety, depression, and other personality and mental problems. Schemas can be helpful in saving people mental energy and quickly conveying a concept. The challenge, of course, is that we do not know the exact schemas that people hold in their minds. The more you know about your audience, the more you will know about their schemas. Some schemas have been found to be consistent across different groups of people. The deep metaphors that we discussed in Chapter 3 are examples of such schemas.

You can activate schemas through the use of metaphors and analogies to help people quickly learn your material. This is especially important when you need to convey complex material in a simple manner. Educational psychologist Richard Mayer conducted an experiment in which he asked two groups of students to perform computer programming problems. One group was provided with an analogy beforehand: "The long-term storage function of the computer was described as a file cabinet; the sorting function was described as an in-basket, save basket, and discard basket on an office desk." When the students attempted to learn to program the language of a database, this analogy didn't make a difference for easy problems, but it made a major difference when the students attempted complex problems. The group of students who had been given the analogy performed twice as well on complex problems versus students who had not been given an analogy.

Consider the level of knowledge that your audience has about your topic. Experts have more developed schemas about their subject areas. They may not need schema prompts to quickly and easily understand your material. People with little background in your field can greatly benefit from the activation of a schema that they already have. When my husband and I were buying our first house, our real estate agent, Jean Zantapolous, in an effort to help us understand the commitment that buying an old house entailed, said, "An old house is like another family member." How can you come up with similar schemas or metaphors to help your clients understand and make the best use of your services?

Simple Is Superior

ACTION STEPS

1. **Set simple goals for yourself.** You might make the goal of your first follow-up call to request to meet for coffee. Then you might make your goal of meeting for coffee to learn more details about someone's business. Simplify your communication and your goals and you'll likely feel calmer and more confident and see better results.

2. **Identify schema.** Listen to the types of things that people talk about, and look for patterns. When you see someone's mood shift, ask yourself what she was just talking about or ask her what she was thinking about. Schemas are often accompanied by specific emotions.

3. **Come up with key analogies.** This is a great way to communicate quickly and succinctly to help people understand your concepts. These analogies and similes can also make great blog posts. For instance, I wrote a post called "Marketing Is Like Gardening."

We've come to the end of this section on deepening your connections by being memorable, following up with excellent value, and stimulating discussion. We're ready to jump into some fun and unique ways to influence people to take action. Let's go!

Part 3

How Do I Influence People to Refer to Me, Hire Me, and Buy from Me?

Chapter 9

Use Social Proof— People Look to Certain Others to Decide What to Do

Picasso once remarked, "I do not care who it is that has or does influence me as long as it is not myself."

—*GERTRUDE STEIN*

A FEW YEARS ago, I was at a wedding in a beautiful historic building in Center City Philadelphia. A 10-piece band that probably cost upward of $15,000 started playing, but no one was dancing. Then a couple spun out onto the floor, elegantly moving across the wood floor in the grand ballroom. After just a couple of minutes, the dance floor was filled, and after a few songs, I didn't see the original dancers anymore. Can you guess what happened? My husband and I figured out that the original couple were professional dancers.

Why would people who have 200 guests attending their wedding hire people to dance? To get others dancing. People have more fun at weddings when they dance, but no one wants to be the first person out on the floor with everyone staring at them. Professional dancers get things going and then others follow.

Wedding dancers are just one of thousands of examples of how we tend to do what other people do. Looking to others to help us decide what to do is called "social proof," and it is one of the most powerful laws of influence. It's the idea of safety in numbers. We are most comfortable making choices when others have made and succeeded with similar choices. This tendency seems to be hardwired and linked with our drive to keep ourselves safe. Our success in business relationships does not on the surface appear to be directly linked with our safety, but subconsciously we know that we need to make good impressions and attract new business in order to keep shelter over our heads, feed our families, and so on. It is frightening to make unprecedented choices and commit to doing business with people if we do not have social proof of their effectiveness.

Because of this, social proof is the strongest of all persuasive principles and one that can help you get results in your business relationships. In this chapter, we'll explore what social proof is and how you can use it help people decide to hire you and refer to you.

Who Are We Most Influenced By?

While we are influenced by those around us, social proof, also called social norms, is particularly powerful when we see the other people as similar to ourselves. In 1954, social psychologist Leon Festinger came up with social comparison theory, which states that we evaluate ourselves by comparing ourselves to people who have similar characteristics to our own.

We can't help but to compare ourselves to others and be influenced by those comparisons. When I walk my dogs down my street and see my neighbors' yards looking beautiful, I feel compelled to work on my own yard. On the other hand, when I'm out in California visiting my sister and I see her neighbors' yards looking beautiful, I appreciate them but do not compare them to my own yard or feel as strongly compelled to work on my yard.

I always ask new clients why now is the time that they want to grow their businesses. A new client recently told me, "I got together with some friends from my grad school class and they all have successful practices, so

I thought, there's no reason I shouldn't have a more successful practice." She's right.

Guests at your hotel

Noted researcher on influence Robert Cialdini and his colleagues Noah Goldstein and Vladas Griskevicius set out to discover exactly how social proof and similarity work. They conducted a fascinating study of hotel room guests to see what type of signs in hotel rooms would most influence guests to reuse their towels and help the environment. The first sign included a message commonly used in hotel rooms that stated how reusing towels helps the environment:

> HELP SAVE THE ENVIRONMENT. *You can show your respect for nature and help save the environment by reusing your towels during your stay.*

The second sign included a social norm statement:

> JOIN YOUR FELLOW GUESTS IN HELPING TO SAVE THE ENVIRONMENT. *Almost 75% of guests who are asked to participate in our new resource savings program do help by using their towels more than once. You can join your fellow guests in this program to help save the environment by reusing your towels during your stay.*

Data were collected in 190 rooms with guests staying at least two nights over 80 days in a midpriced national chain hotel located in the Southwest. The room attendants checked whether guests opted to reuse a towel (by hanging it on a towel rack) versus getting a new one (by leaving the used towel on the floor).

Results showed that people with the social norm statement reused their towel 44 percent more than those with the environmental statement only, an amount much greater than the average towel reuse programs received. This number may even be an underestimate because data were collected only on guests' first eligible day, and the measurement standards were quite strict (e.g., the researchers didn't count towels hung on doorknobs, only on the towel rack). This compelling data highlight how strongly we are influenced by what others do, even when those people have only broad similarities to us, such as being other guests in a hotel.

Guests in the same room of your hotel

These researchers then conducted a modified version of their hotel room study. Because people tend to follow the norms that match their own situations, Goldstein, Cialdini, and Griskevicius theorized that including a social norm statement about the hotel room's previous guests would lead to an even higher rate of towel reuse.

This time they tested five messages:

1. The same as the message on page 139 about general environmental benefit (no social norm).
2. A message about 75 percent of other hotel guests (general social norm).
3. A message that used people who had stayed in the same room as the social comparison group, stating that 75 percent of the guests in that particular room had reused towels.
4. A message that used fellow citizens as the social norm, stating "Join your fellow citizens . . ."
5. A message that specified gender, stating that 76 percent of the women and 74 percent of the men reused their towels.

As the researchers predicted, all of the social norm messages (#2–4) resulted in significantly more towel reuse than the standard environmental message (#1). The message that resulted in the most towel reuse was the similarity message (#3) about people in the same room. This one was statistically higher than the other three (#2, #4, and #5), which were statistically equal to one another.

I would not necessarily think of people who share my same hotel room as being similar to me, but remember that people who share a similar situation or circumstance are a powerful source of social comparison. The more similar the comparison group, the more powerful the influence.

Similarities and your target audience

Your description of current clients should fit with new clients' perceptions of themselves. Remember that people identify strongly with those who are in a similar situation or circumstance to themselves, which can even be as simple as the guests who stayed before you in your hotel room.

When you have a solid understanding of your audience and how they are similar to one another, you can show your understanding of them and use social proof to influence them to hire you or refer to you.

Complete the action steps that follow to ascertain ways in which your target audiences of clients or referral partners are similar to one another, and in the next step we'll explore ways to use social proof in your marketing.

Social Proof and Similarities

ACTION STEPS

1. **Write a list of the fundamental ways that your clients or potential referral partners are similar to each other based on their situation.** For example, a real estate agent may consider her potential clients' similar situations as: first-time home buyers; recently married; looking for short-term (5 to 10 years) home; commute into the city for work. If this real estate agent was focused on marketing to referral partners, rather than clients, she would complete these exercises for how referral partners were similar to one another. If you market to both clients and referral partners, complete a table such as this one:

Similarities	Situation	Demographic	Psychographic
Clients	First-time home buyers, short-term home	Mid-20s to mid-30s, professional, income > $75,000	Pressed for time, motivated to get a good deal, need to move fast

Referral Partner: Loan Officers	Successful, looking to become top performers in their industry	In New York City, work with jumbo loans, work with young professional clients	Needs real estate agent who manages the process and helps clients quickly move through process
Referral Partner: Accountants	Work locally with small businesses and families	Serve clients with income > $75,000, in business for > 10 years	Needs real estate agent who can explain first-time home buying process

2. **Write a list of the fundamental ways that your clients or potential referral partners are similar to one other based on their *demographics*,** including factors such as age, gender, profession, income, education, geography, ethnicity, religion, etc.

3. **Write a list of the fundamental ways that your clients or potential referral partners are similar to one another based on their *psychographics*,** including factors such as motivations, interests, needs, problems, challenges, desires, fears, goals, etc.

The great thing about social proof is that you can use it to create a positive cycle of influence. You use social proof to attract new clients. You then use social proof to enhance the results and benefits your clients receive. You then use social proof from all your great results to attract additional clients and referrals.

Use Similarities to Gain Clients and Referral Partners

Once you have an understanding of who your target audience is most likely to be influenced by, you can create some great tools of social proof. Three of my favorites are testimonials, stories, and visuals.

Testimonials and similarities

You probably already know how powerful testimonials can be in your marketing. They can be very effective—if done in the right way.

As you now know, we're most influenced by others who we perceive as similar to ourselves. This means that it's important to divide your testimonials into groups. You would then utilize the endorsements that best fit the needs of your various specific audiences. For example, if you are a life coach who works with women in career transition, divide your audience, programs, and testimonials into sections, such as "mothers in their late thirties transitioning careers after having children," "midcareer executives in creative fields entering a new industry," and "midcareer executives getting back in the market after being laid off." A real estate agent who serves three counties can segment testimonials by county or by type of home (e.g., new construction or antique charm). A wealth manager can segment by type of client, such as young professionals without children, families with school-age children, or families with children in college or beyond. A yoga studio can divide its marketing materials and testimonials into prenatal yoga, yoga for fitness and weight loss, and yoga for relaxation and spiritual renewal.

You can divide client descriptions and testimonials using any demographic (age, gender, ethnicity, race, geographical location, education, industry, job title, etc.) or psychographic (needs, motivators, goals, interests, etc.) based on the preceding action steps. It is best to segment by the type of client or by a specific benefit that a client needs, rather than doing what most professionals do, which is to divide programs by the type of service offered.

Make sure that you include descriptive information about the person who provides the testimonial so that the people in your audience realize how similar they are to that person. For example, if a niche market that you serve is executives in the design business, you would want to include the following type of information for someone providing a testimonial: "Jane Smith, Chief Operations Officer, Main Line Design, a midsized graphic design firm in the western suburbs of Philadelphia."

If your goal is to attract new referral partners, ask for testimonials from those who have sent you referrals in the past. This may feel odd because the person has already been kind enough to send you clients and now you're asking them for an endorsement as well. You would only do this once you've established a close relationship. Timing is also important—ask your referrer when she and her client have just received the most benefit from your services. Offer a sample testimonial to use, such as, "I've recently referred several clients to (name) for family counseling and they have greatly benefited. The work they have done with (name) has improved their communication skills, enabling me to better address their business financial plan." If you feel uncomfortable asking a referrer for a testimonial, you can accomplish a similar objective with stories (described in the next section).

In addition to making sure that the giver of the testimonial is similar to the receiver of the testimonial (or the clients of the receiver, in the case of referral partners), the content of the testimonial needs to be similar to the content that your ideal client or referral partner needs. The more specific the description of the *results* of your services, the better.

Stories of similarities

Your goal is to paint a clear picture of your target audience and your services when you meet with prospective clients and with referral partners. Doing so helps create a niche for yourself, improves memorability, and activates social proof. A great way to do all these things is through client stories. As we've discussed, stories are one of the best ways to engage people and stimulate action.

One of my colleagues calls these "hip-pocket stories," stories you can bring out and share whenever helpful. If confidentiality is important in your industry, consider creating a few composite stories that protect people's identities but clearly show who's in your market and how they benefit. Keep these stories brief and remember to tell them as stories with a beginning, middle, and end. Include as many visual aids as possible. For example, one of my clients, an image consultant, told the following story:

> I remember a client who came into my office and said, "I need to be on TV next week."
>
> "That's great," I said.

"Well, yes, but look at me. I should be on radio, not TV," he joked.

In his gray pinstriped suit and patterned maroon tie, he looked a bit disheveled and, well, drab. I realized that he was afraid of drawing attention to himself.

"If you're going to be on TV," I said, "you're going to get attention. Let's be sure your image is conveying the message you want."

We immediately went to get him a new suit and hairstyle, and he looked like a million dollars. He took his wife out for dinner that night, and she called to thank me the next day, saying he hadn't looked like that since their wedding day 20 years ago!

Case studies are another great way to tell stories. Be sure to include social norms in your case studies by having a specific case study for every target audience you serve. As with testimonials, you will be sure the right people get the right case studies that they can see themselves in.

As clear as you need to be about who your client is, it is also important to include yourself in the case study. My friend Mark Levy, marketing strategist and founder of Levy Innovation, recommends a process he calls "insight-based case studies." The idea is to put yourself into the story by showing how the solution is one that only *you* could come up with. For example, you might say, "After meeting with Jim, I quickly discovered . . ." rather than just stating the changes that Jim made. This shows how you uniquely come up with solutions, and if Jim is similar to the person hearing the story, you will have used social proof to illustrate how you can help him too. Again, don't forget to tell these as detail-rich, engaging stories rather than as typical, dry, boring case studies. Use adjectives, engage the senses, and create a bit of drama.

Visuals of similarities

My colleague Lynne treats children with anxiety disorders. Toward the beginning of treatment, the child patients are asked to give a name to their worries, such as "the worry bug," and to draw a picture of it. When you walk into Lynne's office, you see dozens of drawings of worry bugs (and other worry creatures) rendered by the little hands of her patients. These drawings wallpaper an entire wall. Some are big; some are small. Some are done in pencil; others are colorfully created in crayon. All are scary. All show that worry affects kids similarly, making them nervous, timid, and anxious. Also on the wall are images of what happens during or after anxiety treatment. In these drawings, worry bugs become small, silly, or squashed. The kid in the drawings becomes big, strong, and happy.

As professional service providers, we often tell our clients that others feel similarly to them or that we've helped others who have issues similar to theirs. This helps people feel that they are not alone and that we have worked with others like them. Imagine the effect, however, if you were a child and you saw an entire wall of illustrations done by kids just like you. You would definitely feel that you weren't weird or unusual or strange to experience worries. You would feel that you were in the right place to get help. And seeing the before-and-after effect of what happens to the worry bugs in just a couple of months would certainly help you feel hopeful, inspired, and perhaps even excited about doing the treatment.

Use Similarities to Gain Clients and Referrals

ACTION STEPS

1. **Ask clients (or referral partners) for testimonials only** *after* they have received a significant benefit from your work—ideally right after.

2. **Be sure that your testimonials show similarity of benefits** that someone achieved (similarity to benefits your prospective client or referral partner desires) and similarity of the situation, demographics, or psychographics.

3. **Divide up your endorsements** and use the ones that best fit each audience in different situations, unless your niche market is extremely narrow, in which case you would use the same endorsements for all.

4. **Have mini-stories ready.** Be ready to tell your stories out loud and also have written case studies.

5. **Create visuals or, better yet, use your clients' visuals.** How can you do something similar to the worry bug example on pages 145–146 to illustrate how your clients feel and the outcomes they achieve?

6. **Ask for referrals and thank clients.** Rather than saying, "I really appreciate referrals," say, "Most of my business is from referrals from previous clients, and I truly appreciate this . . ." Clients will see that other past clients (like themselves) referred and be more likely to do so themselves.

Use Numbers to Gain Clients and Referral Partners

In addition to similarity, another powerful means of social proof is numbers. We trust numbers. We believe that "numbers don't lie." We figure that if many people feel a certain way or do a certain thing, there must be validity in that. If we look on Amazon and see 100 five-star ratings for a book, we assume that it's a great book. If we see 5,000 people following someone on Twitter, we assume that the person writes great tweets. If we see 10,000 fans of a business on Facebook, we assume that business offers valuable products, services, or information. One of my clients was lining up joint ventures for his book launch. In his introductory e-mail, we included a few key numbers that show the magnitude of his audience and how people would benefit from the exposure. He had a 100-percent success rate in which everyone with whom he requested a joint venture said yes.

Quantity versus quality

I tend to prefer a focus on quality versus quantity in marketing materials, but you cannot neglect quantity. For example, a mailing list of 500 loyal subscribers who read everything you write and refer to you is more valuable than a mailing list of 50,000 people who get your e-mails in their spam boxes and never look at them. At the same time, you need to have enough people in your audience because the majority of your subscribers or followers or fans will not be online at any point in time. Those who are may not be ready to buy at that time.

We cannot help but be influenced by numbers. If someone sends an invitation for you to join a social network and you see that only two people are members, you will probably be uninterested. If, on the other hand, people see that you have 1,000 Facebook fans, they will consciously or unconsciously wonder what value people are getting and want to experience it for themselves. A great example of this is how McDonald's restaurants often feature signs that say "Billions and Billions Served," or some such. "Wow," we think to ourselves. "If billions of people like this, it must be good."

What number is a good number?

We are often faced with the decision of whether to show numbers or not. How do you know if your numbers are enough to activate social proof? In many cases, you do not have a choice. For example, people can see how many Twitter followers or LinkedIn connections you have. I would not make numbers for blog post viewers visible if they are very low (such as under 10 or 20 views per post, assuming you post often), and I would not include numbers in an initial partnership request if they were not compelling. One strategy is to combine your different platforms and say, for example, that your social media and e-mail list followings comprise over 10,000 people. Another strategy is to include the platforms of others who have already agreed to partner with you and say, for example, that the combined platforms reach over 100,000.

Use Numbers to Gain Clients and Referral Partners

ACTION STEPS

1. **Review the action steps in Chapter 1 on where to find high-quality connections** and devote a few hours per week to reaching out to new connections.

2. **Build your e-mail list by offering an incentive.** "Sign up for my newsletter" is not an incentive. Instead, offer a specific incentive that people will get when they join, such as a report on "The Top 10 Secretes to..." with something that those in your audience are dying to know.

3. **Once you have more than 1,000 people on your mailing list, let people know.** For example, for my online newsletter, *Stand Out!* I include a statement: "Sent to 13,241 subscribers on the second Tuesday of the month."

4. **Once your blog audience exceeds 10, let people see how many people view or share your blog posts.** People are comforted to know that they aren't wasting their time and view something as valuable when they see that others feel that way as well.

5. **Use specific numbers.** This means that you may need to update things regularly as your numbers change, but it is worth it. People trust and are more compelled by specific numbers, such as 1,007, versus vague numbers, such as "over 1,000."

6. **Conduct creative campaigns for more fans and followers.** For example, my virtual assistant, Raven Howard, recently helped me create a contest in which people wrote their favorite quotes on my fan page wall (you must be a fan to write on the wall), and those whose quotes were my favorites won a prize. We added 103 new fans from this simple and fun contest.

7. **Don't obsess about numbers.** As much as numbers can help, the quality of the material you put out and the relationships that you build are what's most important.

Use Social Proof to Resolve Ambivalence or Objections

Another powerful use of social proof is to address concerns that potential clients or referral partners may have about working with you.

Lessons from long distance drives

One day a client, a busy marketing executive who lived in Delaware, arrived at my office in Philadelphia in a state of irritation. The drive from Wilmington, Delaware, to my office typically takes around one hour but can take longer depending on traffic.

"Are you okay? What's bothering you today?" I asked her.

"It's no big deal, I'll be fine," she told me.

"You don't have to tell me, but I can see that something is upsetting you, and perhaps we could address it quickly and then move on," I suggested.

She told me, "It took me so long to get here today and I have so much to do. No offense, it's not that you're not worth driving all of this way, but it just takes up a lot of time."

"I know, and the traffic on 76 can be horrible, can't it? I have many clients who drive from Delaware and many from New Jersey, and the drive varies so much based on traffic, it's quite frustrating," I said.

"Yeah," my client said, and her mood brightened. "Now, for what we were going to work on today . . ."

Why did her mood shift?

Well, the first and more obvious reason is that she felt empathized with and validated in her frustration. The second and less obvious reason—which you may have guessed now that you know how social proof works—was that she felt better to know that others were doing the same thing she does. Think about it: if you were the only one to drive a long distance to an appointment, you would ask yourself, "Why am I doing this?" Whereas if you knew that others also drove a long distance, you might think, "Well, there's a reason that people are willing to drive so far; I'm in good hands." I learned that I should have directly addressed this concern up front because it could have prevented her from becoming a client, and the social proof that she was not alone in a long commute could have prevented her from becoming frustrated.

Allow others to address ambivalence

Let's say, for example, that you're a financial advisor and you're only 26 years old. You use the ideas you've learned in this book and create some strong business relationships. You could then ask someone who you feel comfortable asking for feedback, "When I first approached you, what made you unsure about working with me?" That person might say, "Well, you just looked and sounded so young." You could respond, "Could you write me a brief endorsement beginning with how you were initially unsure about me because of that?"

When people address the initial skepticism they experienced (and of course the positive result that occurred when they got past it), you have a very powerful form of social proof because others are likely to share the same concerns and be relieved and happy to know that if they put those concerns aside (or address them directly with you), they could receive great benefit from your work together.

Q&A

Another way to address potential concerns about hiring you or referring to you is with a list of common questions and answers. The key to doing this effectively is to know what people's real concerns are rather than making assumptions. You can find out concerns by speaking with people who share the same target market and learning more about the needs of their clients. Let say that you're a graphic designer and your target audience is owners of restaurants. You speak with Web designers, small business accountants, or others who work with restaurant owners and learn more about them. You find out that their biggest challenge is time. One question in your Q&A might be:

Q: *How long will it take from start to finish of my postcard mailings?*
A: We pride ourselves on our fast turnaround time and offer your initial proofs within two business days. Most of our clients receive their final materials within five days and are able to send out a mailing within one week of engaging our services.

Or let's say that you're a motivational speaker and you know from meeting planners that they want to be sure that those in their audience walk away with tangible things they can do differently, not just good feelings. A question in your Q&A might be:

Q: *Are your talks purely motivational?*

A: My style is a combination of motivational and practical. Audience members have called my presentations "inspiring" and also "filled with practical action steps."

Use Social Proof to Resolve Ambivalence or Objections

ACTION STEPS

1. **Directly address or admit to real challenges** of working with you, and let people know how others have navigated that particular challenge.

2. **Create a list of concerns** that your prospective client or referral partner may have about working with you. Conduct research to inform your list.

3. **Address concerns in endorsements from others** who've worked with you in the past. Be sure that you have used the law of social proof and that the person is similar to your prospect.

4. **Address concerns in your Q&A.** These may not be framed as concerns. Be sure to show how others with similar goals benefited in spite of the initial concerns.

Enhancing Outcomes

A final application of social proof is to improve the course of your work with people as well as to inspire new people to hire you and refer to you. The most powerful social proof is real-world results. Your goals are threefold:

1. Serve your clients to the best of your abilities.
2. Create a positive benefit for those who refer to you.
3. Attract new clients.

Helping your clients achieve better outcomes accomplishes all three of these things. Your clients and referral partners benefit, and you have another instance of social proof for the benefits of your services.

Reducing harmful behaviors and increasing helpful behaviors

"Every day, about 3,000 young people put their lives in danger by beginning to smoke cigarettes."

What impact do you think that this statement would have on the reduction of teen smoking?

This statement, similar to what you may see in a common public service announcement, would probably backfire. According to the law of social norms, teenagers considering smoking may embrace the idea that a lot of other teenagers smoke. Instead of thinking, "Smoking is bad," they may think, "Smoking is normal."

Instead, a statement like the following one, found on the National Institute for Drug Abuse Web site (nida.nih.gov) is more likely to reduce teen substance use: "Contrary to popular belief, most teenagers do not use marijuana. Among students surveyed in a yearly national survey, only about one in seven 10th graders report they are current marijuana users (that is, used marijuana within the past month)."

See the difference?

Shine the spotlight

The survival of a park in Arizona, Petrified Forest National Park, has been threatened because visitors take home pieces of petrified wood from the park as souvenirs. To test the impact of the park's signage, Robert Cialdini conducted an experiment similar to the hotel room study he cocreated, but with the goal of decreasing rather than increasing an environmentally friendly behavior.

Two signs were created to be placed along paths in the park. The first addressed social proof: "Many past visitors have removed the petrified wood from the park, changing the natural state of the Petrified Forest."

This sign was accompanied by an image of several people taking the wood.

The second sign said, "Please don't remove the petrified wood from the park, in order to preserve the natural state of the Petrified Forest." This sign had a picture of one person taking a piece of wood with a red circle and bar over his hand.

What do you think happened?

When the researchers compared the impact of these two signs on the amount of wood taken versus a control group that had no sign, they found a dramatic difference: the amount of wood stolen nearly *tripled* in the area where the social proof ("Many past visitors . . .") sign was placed versus the control group with no sign. The second sign, which asked people not to remove wood, slightly reduced the amount of wood taken.

The researchers recommended that park management go a step further and focus their signage on the people who respect the park, showing those who do not that they are in the minority at less than 3 percent. When people feel as though everyone's doing something, they have no problem doing it too, whereas when they feel as though very few people are doing something, they feel that they are in the spotlight and are less likely to do it.

What are the unhelpful behaviors that your clients do that stand in the way of their goals? How can you use social proof to reduce those behaviors?

What are the helpful behaviors that your clients do that facilitate the achievement of their goals? How can you use social proof to increase those behaviors?

Enhancing Outcomes

ACTION STEPS

1. Collect and share data on how people are doing positive things. For example, keep track of client attendance. If you find that 95 percent of your clients come to their regularly scheduled appointments, share this information. If you have intake paperwork, include this data in the section on appointments. When clients keep their appointments, they are likely to see better results more quickly and you are better able to manage your business.

2. **Collect and share data on how people are not doing negative things.** It is usually better to frame your data in the positive, as in #1, but there are times when it makes sense to frame data in the negative to decrease behavior that is not conducive to the client getting optimum results.

3. **Focus statistics on positive changes.** We often share statistics on how many people experience a similar problem. A potential downside is that clients may think, "Hey, if all those people are strong enough to live with this problem, I should be too, so why bother to work on it?" and decide not to get help. People don't typically think these things consciously but are greatly impacted by them. Instead, focus statistics on the people who've received help and benefitted.

Now that you understand the power of social influence with social proof and are committed to the ethical use of it to positively impact your clients and referral partners, let's turn our attention to another powerful law of social influence: reciprocity.

Chapter 10

Give First—
People Naturally Reciprocate
Genuine Support

You can close more business in two months by becoming interested in other people than you can in two years by trying to get people interested in you.

—*DALE CARNEGIE*

WHAT WOULD YOU do if someone bought you a can of Coke?

If you're like the people in a classic experiment by Dennis Regan, you would return the favor. People who had been given a soda from someone bought more raffle tickets from that person than those who had not been given a soda.

It is human nature to reciprocate. The law of reciprocity is powerful. As you'll learn in this chapter, it's about more than feeling indebted to someone. Rather, reciprocity arises from positive feelings and gratitude. Giving can improve your mood, your business bottom line, and even the world. Here's how.

Give When You Mean It

The key to activating the law of reciprocity is that you give something of value from your heart. If you give only in hopes of getting, the law is less powerful and can backfire. Learn more about this principle of spiritual marketing with *The Attractor Factor* and the other great works of Dr. Joe Vitale.

Take a moment to remember a time when you had a fabulous gift to give someone who you care about. You couldn't wait for the occasion to give it to her because you knew she'd love it, and you couldn't wait to see the look on her face. If you are going to give something to someone, this is the mind-set that you need to be in. If you're not in this mind-set and you feel that you're giving away too much or being taken advantage of, the law of reciprocity will backfire. Not only that, but you will waste your valuable time, energy, and money.

Follow first

Consider this scenario: a few weeks ago, someone e-mailed me and said, "Like my Facebook page and then I'll like yours." What effect do you think this had?

Relationships are based on how you make people feel. This message made me feel that the person didn't know anything about me, wasn't interested in my material, and simply wanted new fans for his page. Imagine how different it would have been had he genuinely been interested in my Facebook page (Facebook.com/MarketingPsych), posted several comments there, and then e-mailed me to let me know that he enjoyed my page and let me know about his. At the minimum, I would have gone to his page—something I didn't do after the request he sent me.

A great way to influence people to follow you in social media, sign up for your mailing list, do a joint venture with you, or buy from you is to first do the same for them. One of my clients, an author, told me of his dream to do a joint venture with a well-known author whom he admired. My client had read one of this author's books. I told him to read the rest of his books, buy his products, follow him in social media, and write reviews of his books on Amazon. My client genuinely liked and respected this author, so he was happy to do all of these things, regardless of whether or not a joint venture worked out, though of course we hoped that it would. After learning more about this author's approach, my client realized that the joint venture he had originally anticipated would not be an ideal match, but he had another idea in mind, one that was an excellent fit. When my client approached the author, he was able to genuinely say how familiar he was with his work and how much he liked it.

When you come from a place of true interest, understanding, and admiration, it is easy to give first and mean it. You remain true to yourself and do not feel like you're trying to sell something or feel like you're being manipulative. Remember that the number-one key to attracting more clients is to build authentic relationships.

Discover the icing on the cake

It's hard to study persuasion in the real world. Because of this, much of the research on persuasion has been conducted in university settings. One way to measure persuasion in the real world, however, is through studying tipping in restaurants. I waited tables for 10 years during undergraduate and graduate school, and I always enjoyed learning about the impacts of my service on customers' tipping. I joke that I learned more about human behavior by working in restaurants than I did while completing a doctorate in psychology—and it's only partly a joke. One lesson I learned was that you can't predict who will be good tippers. Often the people who you might think would tip well would not and vice versa. This is an argument for not stereotyping and providing your best possible service no matter what.

That said, a few things have been found to influence customer tipping behavior. On top of excellent service, these things can be the icing on the cake. Servers who receive higher tips introduce themselves by name, mirror the type of communication style that customers show, and draw images (such as a happy face or American flag) on checks. Some of these factors (such as drawing the happy face) have held more true for female servers than for males servers. Nonverbal communication such as smiling, touching a customer's shoulder, or crouching to eye level with the customers also tend to increase tipping. What is the icing in your business? It may be a check-in call between meetings, a personal thank-you card, professional use of touch (handshake, shoulder touch), or something else. The eye-level finding is interesting because being at the same eye level equalizes the perception of power, which makes people feel more comfortable. Women tend to feel more comfortable when their eye level is slightly higher than the other person's.

Little gifts that make a big difference

Giving a little gift can go a long way. Back to studies of tipping in restaurants: When servers gave each of their customers a small piece of candy with the check, they earned 3.3 percent more in tips. When they gave two pieces of candy per customer, they earned a staggering 14 percent more in tips. What a return on investment for a couple pieces of candy!

It amazes me how people are reluctant to give little gifts because they don't want to spend the money. They'll spend $50 to go to a networking event and then not follow up with the people they meet. They won't spend $12 to buy a book or take someone to lunch. They won't spend $3 to send a card. It's these smaller things—things that are perceived as receiving little gifts—that make a big difference.

The way to select little gifts that make a big difference is to make sure that they are:

- **Scarce.** Scarcity is another powerful social influence tool. You see marketers try to use the scarcity principle all the time by saying things like "limited time offer" and "while supplies last"; some of these pitches work well and some are blatant sales gimmicks.

    Two things I like to send out are cards and cookies or candy—things that people universally enjoy. Don't send cookies or candy to someone who you know is on a diet, but if you don't know, don't worry about it; they can always enjoy sharing the treats with others, plus moderation rather than deprivation is linked with long-term weight loss success, but that's another story.

    When do you think I avoid giving these things out? If you guessed during the holidays, you are right. There are cards and cookies everywhere, so the small gift has a small impact rather than the big impact we'd like.

- **Relevant.** The more timely something is, the better. If I sent out a tool for organizing your tax paperwork in August, it would be irrelevant to most people for many months. They would be dealing with back-to-school shopping, end of summer travel, and other such things, so my gift would have little relevance.
- **Thoughtful.** You've heard, "It's the thought that counts." It is true. What influences people more than what you get them is the thought that you put into it. Deliver your gifts with a message like, "I remembered you saying how much you enjoy reading leadership books so I thought you'd enjoy this one; it's one of my favorites."

Give When You Mean It

ACTION STEPS

1. **Follow those who interest you.** If you don't use Twitter, go to whichever social media you use and make a point to follow those in whom you have a genuine interest. If you're on both Twitter and Facebook, post on Facebook for people to share their Twitter handles (and then follow them). When they write on your wall, you increase your exposure and forge a connection.

2. **Share your thoughts.** Comment on people's blog posts and Facebook pages. Join LinkedIn groups and share your thoughts. When the ideas you share are of high value, you will activate the law of reciprocity.

3. **Send a card.** Printed cards tend to be more powerful than e-mail since they're less common these days. The fast and easy service I use to send is SendOutCards.com. Or buy a package of beautiful cards or have cards with your logo designed, and get in the habit of sending them out regularly.

4. **Ask yourself, "How can I provide even better service?"** This can be something as small as writing a personal thank-you on your invoice

slips, bringing dessert to a lunch meeting, giving a call to your clients in between meetings to see how they're doing, and so on.

5. **Give two monthly gifts.** Budget $25 a month to give two gifts in the $12 range, such as books to people who you appreciate working with.

6. **Be aware of personal space.** Do not come closer than 18 inches. Arrange your office so that chairs are about three to four feet apart—any closer and you can invade personal space; any farther and you can lose connection. Set chair heights so that you see eye to eye with clients. If your clients are mostly women, set their chair height slightly higher.

Give Thought to Your Opening

I'm often asked how much courtship and conversation is good and when it's better to get right to a request. One of the primary considerations is your business partner. Follow her lead. If she tends to speak in a direct style, speaks quickly, has a fairly serious businesslike demeanor, and is a cut-to-the-chase type, it is probably better to get to the point quickly. Your gift to her is time. If, on the other hand, she seems to place emphasis on relationships and conversation, connection is most important. As I discuss in more detail in *The Confident Leader*, there are three essential types of motivation: (1) achievement, (2) power and leadership, and (3) affiliation or social motivation. Figure out what motivates your referral partners and prospective clients. The first two (achievement and power) suggest cutting to the chase, and the third (affiliation) suggests spending some more time talking. Here are some other factors to consider, brought to light in recent research. . . .

When to chat

One of my clients, Robert, a mortgage broker, became good at using the relationship-building skills we've discussed thus far, and his marketing became very effective. He had a nice flow of prospective clients.

Sometimes, however, he avoided calling people because he did not like to ask people for business. I gave him an unusual exercise:

"Robert," I said, "I want you to write down everything you'd say in your sales monologue and call me back in five minutes."

"Uh, okay," he said, part confused, part curious.

When he called back, I pretended that I was a client and had him read his script to me. As expected, it didn't go well.

"Okay, hang up the phone. Then rip it up," I advised. "Call me back and chat with me for a few minutes, and then ask a question to open up the discussion about your products."

When he did this, he had a completely different demeanor. We chatted for a bit. Then he asked me about my needs and described a product and asked some more questions. The conversation went back and forth like a Ping-Pong match.

"What was different?" I asked him.

"I don't know," Robert said. "I guess it felt like the pressure was off, and I felt more like myself."

This is not to say that you don't want to be prepared for calls or even to have scripts or notes to refer to as long as you use them flexibly. What you don't want is to deliver a lot of information at once in a speech-like way. In an interesting article called "Dialogue Involvement as a Social Influence Technique," Polish researchers Dariusz Dolinski, Magdalena Nawrat, and Izabela Rudak describe how people are more likely to take desired action when a request is preceded by a casual dialogue rather than by a monologue. This effect may be because of the way people communicate. We tend to engage in more of a dialogue with friends and a monologue with strangers. When we engage in a dialogue, we may feel similarly to how we feel with a friend, which makes us comfortable. We tend to be more influenced by friends than strangers, so feeling like we do with friends makes us more likely to be influenced by that person even if that person is a stranger.

When, however, someone already is your friend, the reciprocity law may not be as strong. Recall the example at the beginning of the chapter about how people were more likely to purchase raffle tickets from a stranger who had bought them a soda. In 1995, a group of researchers discovered that the reciprocity effect did not hold true if the person who bought you the soda was a friend. People bought more raffle tickets after having received a favor from strangers but not after having received a favor from a friend. When a friend made a request, it did not matter whether or not they had first done a favor for you. So save your money if the person you're trying to influence is a friend (just kidding). This stranger versus friend effect may exist because with friendships, you have a longer time perspective. You know that eventually you help each other out and reciprocate down the line.

Thus it may be that you don't actually need to *be* friends with someone to influence them, but you need to *communicate* as though you were friends—in a conversational dialogue.

When to get to the point

Typically, when we tell a story, we share a beginning that may include background information, and the story builds to some form of punch line or natural conclusion. Consider, on the other hand, how news stories are presented. The lead or the most important part typically comes first. For example, on Yahoo! right now there is a story with the headline "8 Reasons Carbs Help You Lose Weight." The first two sentences are: "Eating a diet packed with the right kind of carbs is the little-known secret to getting and staying slim for life. When we talk about the right kind of carbs, we mean Resistant Starch . . ." The article gets right to the point. We get pulled in and then continue reading. Look over the news headlines today and you'll see how many headlines and first few sentences use this technique of leading with the lead. We respond well to it because we're pressed for time and we want to know the important information right away.

Lead with the lead, like a news article, when you don't have a lot of time to influence someone, when you need to have maximum impact, when you need to grab attention, or when you know that someone's highest values are time and the bottom line. Also consider the person who you want to influence—the best way to influence behavior is to change it in yourself first. If you're speaking with someone who tends to talk in circles before getting to the point, model the behavior that you'd like to see from them. Use the "bottom line technique" and help them pace themselves to get to the point more quickly.

Give Thought to Your Opening

ACTION STEPS

1. **Discover people's motivation.** Pay attention to what seems to motivate the people with whom you do business: achievement (intellectual, success, financial), power (leadership and authority), or affiliation (social and relationships).

2. **Mirror communication style.** Go for a more direct or a more chatty approach based on the other person's communication style. Either way, employ the dialogue skill that involves a conversational style and some conversation before making your request.

3. **Write three articles that lead with the lead.** These articles will give value in a way that respects people's time. Include these articles in the keep-in-touch marketing plan we discussed in the last section.

Give without Giving Everything Away

When I first learned about the principle of reciprocity and its application to marketing, I began to give everything away: my products, my time (to do interviews), my ideas, and so on. At first, I saw excellent results. The more people learned about my ideas, presumably the more ready they were to hire me, and I got a decent stream of new clients and referrals. After a certain point, I was working a ton, including evenings and weekends, but I wasn't earning as much or enjoying my work as much as I should have been. I realized that I was giving too much away and neglecting to build a profitable business.

Do you make this mistake too? It looks something like Figure 10.1. The problems with giving too much away include:

- "Why buy the cow when you can get the milk for free?" People won't hire you or buy from you if they get everything they need for free.

Figure 10.1 Optimal Amount Given Away

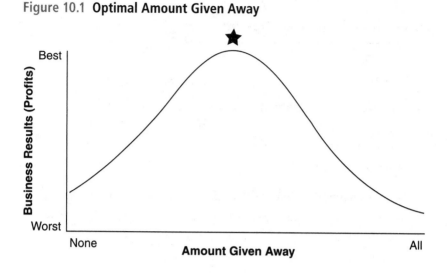

- You don't have time to create tons of material to give away *and* provide the best quality service to your clients *and* have a great quality of life for yourself.
- You can be overexposed. Recall the scarcity law of influence. If your products are everywhere, they can be seen as less scarce and therefore less valuable.
- You undermine your confidence and neglect to charge what you are worth. If you're used to saying "free," stating your fee can be a big leap.

So, how do you find that happy medium? It will take some experimenting and getting to know your audience. You'll begin to see where and how you can best leverage your time. The key is the quality of exposure and focus of the audience. The higher quality the exposure outlet and the more narrow the audience, the better.

If you find that some people with whom you have business relationships are "takers" (they constantly ask you to do things for free for them or their audience), don't hesitate to ask for what you need. They may not realize that you aren't getting the benefit that you want or need or may not know how to provide it. Reciprocity can be misunderstood—if you aren't getting benefits, make your needs known, and if the relationship remains unbalanced, move on to something else.

Give without Giving Everything Away

ACTION STEPS

1. **Fill in the blank: Right now, the way I feel about what I give away in my business is** _____. Pay attention to the emotion that comes up for you. If you feel frustrated, drained, or unappreciated, you are probably giving away too much. If you feel tightfisted, closed, or skeptical, you are probably giving away too little. If you feel generous, abundant, and satisfied, you are probably giving away the right amount.

2. **Give away the first part.** Take something that has a lot of value (a product or service that you offer) and give away just a small part. The key to making this strategy work is that the small part must have complete value on its own. If it leaves people hanging, they will be frustrated, which obviously is the last thing you want. Think of it like a small appetizer before a meal. It is delicious and complete but leaves people wanting more.

3. **Be especially careful with giving away your time.** In the coaching industry, it's common to give away free coaching sessions. I don't advise this. Give away interviews, audios, and other things to help people get to know you without giving away your time. If you don't value your time, how can you expect someone else to?

4. **Give in order to "book yourself solid."** In his bestselling book *Book Yourself Solid*, Michael Port discusses how to create a funnel of giveaways and paid products and services to move people through a process beginning with free and moving up to your premium product or service. If you simply give without a system in place, you are unlikely to get new business. He also discusses who to give to—those who pass your "red velvet rope policy" and are your ideal clients.

Give Compliments and Concessions

It's simple: compliments make us feel good. And concessions make us feel like we're getting something or getting out of something easily, which makes us feel good. Here's how . . .

How to give compliments

Have you ever been given a compliment that feels forced or insincere? This feels horrible. The first and foremost thing is that you are sincere in giving compliments. If you do not typically express your feelings, your compliment may be sincere, but you may come across as insincere because you are uncomfortable. It takes practice. Begin by complimenting those who you're most comfortable with, and work your way up to more difficult situations.

Another important characteristic of compliments that have a positive impact is that they are specific. The best thing to compliment is something that is within someone's control. Let's say that you go to a potential referral partner's office, which she shares with several colleagues in her practice. Rather than compliment something in the waiting room (which may or may not be her doing), compliment something in her office. Be careful not to compliment something that people can't easily replicate, like one of my friends did; I have naturally curly hair. When I have the time—which is about as often as it snows in Florida—I straighten it. One day, I made the time to straighten my hair, and my husband and I went out with friends for dinner. My friend said, "Oh, I love your new hairstyle! It looks so much better!" "Oh great," I thought. "How bad do I look every day? It won't look like this again for another three months!" Have you ever had something like this happen to you? It's not good.

To be specific, compliments must be customized to the individual. Let's go back to tipping in restaurants to learn more about this. In a 2010 study, researchers went into four restaurants (two were major franchises) and observed 360 dining parties ranging from 1 to 17 people. The servers (two male and two female) were asked to wait tables as they normally would but to give a compliment to randomly determined tables, while the other tables received no compliments. Servers complimented diners on their meal choices after they ordered by saying, "You both made good choices" to parties of two, and "You all made good choices" to parties of more than two. Servers recorded their tips, and total check amounts and tip percentages were calculated. Compliments in general increased servers' tips by 3.1 percent, but there was an interesting twist—compliments increased tips only with parties of three or fewer diners. Compliments made no difference in parties of four diners, and compliments actually decreased tips with parties of five or more. The sex of the server did not make a difference. Another interesting finding is that one of the four servers received lower tips when she provided compliments. The researchers theorized that she was less verbally expressive, so perhaps people saw her compliments as not genuine. Without her data, the overall increase in tips for the other three servers was 4 percent when they provided compliments. The researchers explain the increases in tips when servers complimented diners as being due to an increase in likeability and perhaps the principle of reciprocity.

Progress down the hill rather than up

In his groundbreaking book *Influence,* Robert Cialdini tells a funny and poignant story: Walking down a street one night, he was approached by a Boy Scout who asked if he'd like to buy a ticket to their circus that Saturday evening. Cialdini declined and the Boy Scout said, "If you don't want to buy any tickets, how about buying some of our chocolate bars? They're only $1 each." Cialdini observed: "(a) I do not like chocolate bars. (b) I do like dollars. (c) I was standing there with two of his chocolate bars. (d) He was walking away with two of my dollars."

Cialdini was fascinated by what had happened; he and his research team decided to explore the phenomenon further. They devised a study in which college students were approached on campus and asked if they wanted to volunteer to take a group of "juvenile delinquents" to the zoo. No surprise—83 percent of students declined. Other college students were also asked this same question, but first they were asked if they would volunteer to work with "juvenile delinquents" for two hours a week for two years. Of those who were first presented with this more extreme request, 50 percent agreed to the zoo day. Three times as many people agreed to the smaller request if they were first presented with a larger request.

How can you apply the concession effect to your marketing?

When presenting your programs, begin by presenting your larger, more expensive program. If a prospect is not interested, you can move to the next program and activate the concession effect. You will also achieve the benefit of psychological anchoring. Anchoring occurs when we get something in our mind and it frames how we see other things. If a consultant typically charges $300 an hour, we see her as a $300-an-hour consultant even if we get a discount. We feel grateful that we are getting a great deal. As long as your initial anchor or offer is reasonable for your profession, your background, and your practice, concessions can work nicely. Do not mark something way up only to mark it down—people are savvy to this tactic and don't like it. Also, do not get in the habit of giving concessions every time, or you will never sell any of your higher ticket items, and you may psychologically undermine the value of what you offer.

Give Compliments and Concessions

ACTION STEPS

1. **Practice giving compliments.** If you are not in the habit of doing so in both your personal and professional lives, it will feel awkward at first and will take some practice.

2. **Select a specific, repeatable attribute or behavior to compliment.** When possible, share how a particular attribute or behavior impacted you. For example: "I was really moved by your personal story of how you got into the work that you do" or "Your comment brightened my day."

3. **Give public displays of gratitude.** Praise people for their ideas and work in front of their coworkers. Leave compliments on people's social media pages. It feels great to get compliments and even better when others hear them.

4. **Aim for the moon when pricing and packaging your services.** There's a Willis Reed quote I like: "Go for the moon. If you don't get it, you'll still be heading for a star."

5. **List prices even if you're giving something for free.** If you call something "free," that is the perceived value. If, however, you say that it is $49, our minds will anchor it there, and it will feel like a great value if someone gets it for free.

6. **List original prices and the discount.** Similar to the above, seeing an original price in writing anchors the value, and then we see the benefit of the deal we receive. I typically see the dollar difference as more powerful than the percentage. Saving $150 feels more powerful to me than saving 10 percent.

Give Gratitude

Adam Smith once wrote, "The sentiment which most immediately and directly prompts us to reward, is gratitude."

Getting in the habit of feeling and expressing gratitude is good for your business, your health and well-being, and for society. So what exactly is gratitude, and why does it move us to act for the betterment of both ourselves and others?

Gratitude is expressing appreciation for a benefit you received. Gratitude has been the subject of a great deal of recent research in the positive psychology movement and has been linked with improved mood and sleep, reduced stress, and enhanced satisfaction with relationships, work, and life.

Gratitude is viral

Michael McCullough and colleagues at the University of Miami propose that gratitude helps us determine benefits in situations, increases the likelihood that we'll behave in helpful ways in the future, and motivates us to help others. Interestingly, gratitude extends the law of reciprocity because it also motivates people to help strangers who have not done something for them. Researchers Monica Y. Bartlett and David DeSteno published a study in 2006 that showed that when people felt grateful toward someone, they helped that person more, even on a dry and boring task. They were also more likely to help a stranger than were people who hadn't experienced gratitude.

Getting into a grateful mind-set can also stimulate trust. Jennifer R. Dunn and Maurice E. Schweitzer from the University of Pennsylvania conducted a study that found that gratitude created a higher level of trust toward a third party (who was not involved in the feeling of gratitude) than when people thought about a time in which they were angry, guilty, or proud. Recall our earlier discussion of how trust builds relationships and enhances influence.

What really influences people?

Ryan Goei and his colleagues conducted two experiments to see what really influences people to take action: favors, apologies, gratitude, or liking. In the first study, 64 female university students were told that they were going to participate in a creativity experiment along with another student. The other student was actually a confederate. The participant and confederate sat in the room with the examiner and did three-minute brainstorming exercises. When they were done, the examiner told the two people (one participant, one confederate) that she would be back in two minutes and asked them not to talk. When she returned, a second brainstorming task was completed. The examiner left again, but before she did, the confederate asked, "While you're doing that, can I get a quick drink?" The examiner responded, "Sure, but don't be long."

One group of confederates returned quietly. Another group came back with a bottle of water and said sincerely to the participant, "Oh, I should have bought one for you too. That was stupid. I'm sorry." They were apologizing for a transgression they didn't really make since people wouldn't expect a bottle of water. A third group brought a second bottle of water and said, "Here you go, I bought one for you too." These people were providing a favor. A fourth group gave the same apology as the one above but then went and got a second bottle and said, "Here you go."

Everyone completed another brainstorming task. The examiner then asked them to complete a survey that measured how much the participant and confederate reported liking one another. They all did a final brainstorming task, and the examiner again asked them not to talk as she left. The confederate asked, "If we can't talk at all, is it okay if I give her a note that doesn't have anything to do with the experiment?" The experimenter responded, "That's okay. But please, do not talk at all." The confederate wrote a note that read: "Hey, I'm selling raffle tickets for my old high school. The tickets cost $1.00 each and the prize is a new iPod. If you are willing to buy any, would you just write how many on this note and give it back to me right away so I can make out the tickets after." Participants wrote how many they wanted to buy on the paper and returned it to the confederate. The participants were then given a partial debriefing by the examiner and were told that the other person was part of the study and had been asked to make the request for raffle tickets. They were not told that the favor and apology incidents were part of the study. The participants completed a survey about why they complied with the raffle ticket request.

The results showed several interesting things. First, the favor increased a sense of gratitude but did not influence reports of liking. Second, the apology increased liking. Third, liking had no effect on compliance. Fourth, gratitude had a substantial (just under statistically significant) effect on compliance. The researchers concluded that the favor increased compliance probably due to a sense of gratitude.

We'd think that liking someone would make us more apt to comply with her, or that a favor would make us like someone more, but neither proved true in this study. To learn more, the experimenters conducted a second study to see what would happen if the request were more self-serving and if the apology were for a true transgression. In the first experiment, the raffle ticket request served to benefit a school. What would happen if the person simply wanted to earn money and made a self-serving request? In this experiment (which included both men and women), the confederates received a cell phone call. They answered it loudly and distracted the participant. Later on, they apologized for this. The confederate who gave a favor returned with two bottles of water as in the first study. This time the confederate made the self-serving request, "Hey, I'm selling raffle tickets, and if I sell enough tickets I win $50, and I could use it. I'm just taking pledges, so you don't need any money right now. They're $1.00 each and the winner gets $300. Think you could help me out?"

The results of this second study showed that the favor had a substantial effect on both gratitude and liking. This time, liking influenced compliance but gratitude did not.

Taking both studies together, we learn that a favor has a positive effect on compliance. We comply with a request more if someone has done a favor for us. Indebtedness does not impact compliance. This shows that reciprocity is different from indebtedness and that reciprocity is more due to positive emotions and gratitude. Feeling gratitude toward someone increases the likelihood that you'll respond to a request, whereas feeling indebted to someone does not.

Apology has a positive effect on liking in both studies, even if you're apologizing for not giving a favor (as in the first study). If you're making a general prosocial request, gratitude is a stronger predictor of compliance than liking. But if you're making a request that directly serves you rather than a social good, liking becomes more important than gratitude or other factors.

We like those who like us

The types of requests (e.g., for sales) that you will be making are likely somewhere in the middle of the two just described in the previous study. In the first study, the request was associated with a social benefit (a school). In this case, gratitude was more important than liking. In the second study, the request was associated with a personal benefit (earning money). In this case, liking is more important than gratitude. Why would we want to support someone we don't like?

In our work, we receive a benefit but so does our client. To be on the safe side, why not employ both liking and gratitude? The good news is that you can easily achieve both with one simple thing: *Tell people how you appreciate them.* We like those who like and appreciate us. When you thank your clients, customers, and business partners, go beyond saying, "We appreciate your business." Recall the effect of size on effectiveness of compliments; when a compliment is given in a generic way or to too large of a group, it can have no effect or even an adverse effect. Instead, personalize your expression of gratitude. The more personal it is, the greater likelihood people will feel that you truly like and appreciate them; the law of reciprocity will be activated, and they will feel the same about you.

Don't limit your expressions of appreciation to people for having their business. Share your gratitude for the process of working with them and for them as people. For example, a divorce attorney might say to a client, "I understand how difficult this process is, and appreciate how well you are handling it. I can tell you are dedicated to your children and to making this as easy as possible on all of you." A financial planner might say, "I can see that you value providing for your family and am honored to help you create the financial planning program to help you do that."

Give Gratitude

ACTION STEPS

1. **Begin a daily gratitude journal.** Write down three things that you're grateful for each day. Foster your grateful mind-set and you're likely to see many positive effects in both your work and life.

2. **Say this sentence: "I appreciate _____ because _____."** This is a step beyond saying thank you and shows people how you really took note of their actions.

3. **Look for small ways to do favors.** You will be more influential if you've done a favor for someone. Look for little things to do, like paying someone's parking meter before a business meeting, holding a door (this is not just for men), or getting someone a bottle of water.

4. **Apologize if you can't do a favor—even if you weren't asked to do a favor.** Recall that when people apologized for not bringing a bottle of water for someone else (even though that person hadn't requested one), that person reported liking them more. Liking is particularly important if your request directly benefits you rather than society in general.

5. **Provide gratitude for the process before making a request.** You may say to a prospective client, "I've enjoyed our conversation and appreciate having gotten to know more about (insert something specific you've learned). I would enjoy the opportunity to help you (insert their specific goal)."

6. **Establish an appreciation program.** You might have one for referrals and another one for clients and customers. Think of it like a frequent flyer program. For instance, they get something valuable after five referrals.

7. **Express gratitude for collaboration.** This goes along with giving a compliment. Let's say that you and another professional are both working with a client and you've found that the other professional's work has really helped the client. You can let that person know how you appreciate the way they've helped the client as well as the opportunity to collaborate with them.

Give Back

In the book *Marketing Lessons from the Grateful Dead* (a great read, especially if you're a Grateful Dead fan like I am), authors David Meerman, Scott Halligan, and Brian Halligan explain how the Grateful Dead gave back through benefit concerts for 20 years and then established the Rex Foundation as a nonprofit organization, which has granted $8.5 million to charities. Most of us cannot give back at this level, but how can you give back to your community in a meaningful way? You, your brand, your clients, and your community will all benefit.

Now that you have activated two of the most powerful social influence practices—social proof and reciprocity—you want to be sure that someone will take action on your service or product offering. One of the most important factors is the clarity and simplicity of your offer. Let's explore that now.

Chapter 11

Simplify Everything— People Deliberate on the General and Act on the Specific

---

Simplicity is the ultimate sophistication.

—LEONARDO DA VINCI

KATHLEEN, A CAREER coach, was wrapping up an excellent presentation. The audience had responded beautifully throughout—asking questions and showing interest. She knew that she had to include some sort of call to action so that people would follow up with her or hire her. So she said, "If you'd like to learn more, you can get my free report, 'Shifting Career Gears,' on my Web site, or $50 off my career tune-up session, or a full career overhaul package, discounted by 20 percent for those who've attended this session." People were enthralled with her for 60 minutes, but she lost the opportunity to get people to take action at the end. Do you know why?

It's simple: the choices she offered were not simple.

People had to think about what they might want. They had to make a choice. "But," you may be thinking, "isn't choice a good thing?" Choice

177

empowers. Choice gives options. Choice gives control. Choice gives freedom. "And what if I give only one option but people don't want that one? Wouldn't I lose the person?" I hear that one a lot. These things are true. Choice can, however, lead to another thing: paralysis.

When Kathleen came to me for marketing strategy and speech coaching, she told me about the situation I just described. One hundred qualified prospects attended her talk. Most seemed interested. Almost all gave her stellar ratings on her feedback form. Yet she did not enroll any new clients. The reason, as you now know, was the choices she gave. People didn't take action.

Choice can be a good thing or a bad thing. Decades of psychological research support the benefits of choice. Choice increases the perception of control, which enhances mood, motivation, and performance. As helpful as choice can be, there are times when it hinders rather than helps your marketing efforts. Let's explore what works and what doesn't work in giving people choices about your service offerings. We'll also explore how people choose—to ensure that they choose you over other service providers.

Why People Buy

Sheena S. Iyengar of Columbia University and Mark R. Lepper of Stanford University conducted a study of jam shopping at an upscale grocery store in California. They set up a jam tasting booth that displayed either 6 or 24 varieties of jam to see what consumers were more attracted to and if there was a difference in purchasing behavior. Shoppers were 62 percent female and 38 percent male. The 24 jams included exotic flavors and did not include traditionally popular flavors such as strawberry. To be sure that the 6 jams weren't jams that people would prefer and skew the results, the researchers did a survey of Stanford students beforehand and asked them to rate the 24 jams from most to least preferred. They selected two of the most preferred (kiwi and peach), two moderately preferred (black cherry and three-fruits), and two least-preferred (lemon curd and red currant). This process ensured that the 24- and 6-jam displays included jams of equal preference level.

Shoppers encountered one of the displays (they were rotated hourly) and were advised to try as many jams as they'd like. They received a $1 off coupon that could be used for one week and could purchase by going to the jam shelf, selecting the jam, and paying for it at the register with their groceries. Purchases were measured by a code on the coupon (disguised as a scanning code), which indicated whether the person had encountered 6 or 24 jams.

Initial attraction was measured by observing how many people stopped at the display. For the display of 24 jams, 242 people encountered the display and 145 people (60 percent) stopped. For the display of 6 jams, 260 people encountered the display and 104 (40 percent) stopped. People were more attracted to the extensive display of 24 jams than the display of only 6 jams. There was no significant difference in the number of jams people sampled at the 6- or 24-jam displays; on average, people sampled two jams. So what did people buy? The results were striking: 31 people (30 percent) who encountered the 6 jams purchased, whereas only 4 people (3 percent) of those who encountered 24 jams purchased a jar of jam. The 24 jams were more attractive and aroused more curiosity, but perhaps the people who stopped at the display of 6 were different in some way than those who stopped at 24.

When my husband and I were selling our condo, I got really into staging it for the open house. I hired cleaners, bought flowers, set the table, the works. My real estate agent cautioned me not to get my hopes up too high, though, because she said that few homes are sold on the basis of an open house. Why might this be? Often people who attend open houses are like those who are attracted to the table of 24 jams. They drive by and see a sign and have a few minutes, so they stop in. They scroll through dozens of houses online and see that one has an open house, so they stop by. Curiosity-seekers, they are sometimes called. What about the serious house hunters? They may be more like the people who stop at the display of 6 jams—more ready to purchase. They have an agent, they've met criteria, and they are ready to purchase. What does this mean for your business? Two things:

- Get specific and limit the options.
- Find the people who are ready to purchase.

Here's how.

Get specific and limit the options

The results of the jam study indicate that too many choices leads to inaction. In this case, 6 choices was far superior to 24 choices. Much of the previous psychological research on choice found that choice can be a good thing. In these studies, participants typically had two to six options from which to choose. We can infer from all of this that six or fewer options is ideal. So how do you limit your clients' choices? Here are some examples to get you thinking:

- **A coach** can offer three specific programs from which a client can choose.
- **A salesperson can present** one particular new product at a time.
- **A speaker or trainer** can have one signature program that is offered in three formats: one hour, four hours (half day), eight hours (full day).
- **A consultant** can offer two outcome-based programs, such as one for teambuilding and one for a leader's emotional intelligence.
- **A psychologist** can offer treatment for three particular disorders.
- **A real estate agent** can specialize in two neighborhoods.
- **A financial advisor** can present two strategic options to her clients.
- **An attorney** can offer four services; for example, an intellectual property attorney can offer copyright consultation, trademarks, service marks, and patents.
- **A massage therapist** can offer three types of services: carpal tunnel therapy, deep tissue massage, and sports massage.
- **An accountant** can offer three fee-capped packages: one for an individual who has a job, one for small business owners, and one for married couples (clients could be charged less than the fee cap if their needs are less).

What can you do to simplify and limit the service offerings that you provide?

If it's possible with your line of work, another tool to simplify your services and enhance the perception of value is to package them. Ideally, package them based on the end result that people will receive. For example, one of my clients, an accountant and financial consultant to small businesses, and I packaged his programs into:

- Shave 20 percent or more off your overhead expenses.
- Get paid on time and do away with your account receivables.
- Make the most of your tax deductions.

As you can imagine, new clients were more likely to sign up for a program with a specific benefit than to receive an intangible, general benefit such as "financial consulting." Additionally, clients were willing to pay more to receive one of these benefits because they could quickly mentally calculate the return on investment of saving 20 percent off overhead versus the investment in consulting. They felt the pain of not being paid on time and were happy to hire someone who can alleviate this pain. And they disliked that uneasy and unsure feeling about whether they were doing the best they could with their tax deductions and were eager to resolve that issue.

Professionals sometimes say that they're concerned to package their services together because a big number is more threatening to prospective clients than a small number. For example, a $2,000 program is more distasteful than $200 per hour. This can be true, but there are several key factors to consider:

- **The fear of the unknown.** For most people, the unknown holds more fear than the known. This is why people stay in bad jobs, relationships, and so on. I would prefer to know that I would need to spend $2,000 and budget for that than to worry that invoices for $200 per hour would pile up to an unknown amount.
- **Conflict of interest.** Prospective clients sometimes worry about paying someone by the hour. An inherent conflict of interest arises because the service provider gets paid more the slower he or she goes. Most ethical professionals work as quickly as possible in spite of this, but this conflict of interest can be real or at least real in the minds of clients.

- **How much your client earns per hour.** If your client also provides fee-for-service hourly services, she will mentally calculate the difference, and if you charge more than she does, this will be unsettling to her. It feels like a loss of money. There is an economic theory called loss aversion put forth by Amos Tversky and Daniel Kahneman that shows that people strongly prefer to avoid losing money over the potential of gaining money. If you charge more than your clients, help them not experience loss aversion by packaging your services. This creates an apples to oranges comparison rather than apples to apples, which makes them feel that they are losing money.

- **Lead with the benefit.** Packaging your services allows you to promote the benefit rather than the service. Clients hire you to receive a benefit. They don't necessarily care about the process or how they will get there. A couple goes to a marriage counselor because they want a better marriage. A client goes to an accountant because she can't stand doing her accounting and wants to be sure everything is done correctly. A patient goes to a chiropractor because he wants his neck pain to go away. A client goes to a wellness coach because she wants to lose weight, gain energy, and have more balance in her life. A client hires a virtual assistant to help make her e-mail marketing more effective by managing her e-mail list and creating her e-zines. A client goes to a social media consultant because he doesn't want to waste his time in social media and wants to attract new business. A couple hires an interior designer to create a beautiful, warm, and inviting living space for their family . . . You get the idea. Clients hire service professionals for the benefits that they will receive.

- **People buy specific and ponder general.** Putting your services into programs makes your services more specific. Think about this: When was the last time you bought a shirt? Truth is, you never really purchased a generic "shirt." You've bought a great striped non-iron button-down that you can throw on and be out of the door to meet with a client in five minutes. You've bought a beautiful bright blue shirt that brings out the color of your eyes. You've bought a great lightweight white shirt to wear outside when it's hot. You've bought a tee with the name of your alma mater broadly displayed on the front. But you've never bought just a shirt. If you were to think of buying a shirt, you would deliberate. What color? What material? What purpose? What style? If, however, you were to think about buying a new white dress shirt to go under your pinstriped suit, you'd know exactly what to do and would buy it when you found it.

Is it possible to group your services together into packages? If so, great, go for it! Just keep the packages to six or fewer. If not, you can create crystal clear benefits about your services so that people know exactly what they're getting and will be ready to buy.

Find the people who are ready to purchase

Referral relationships are my favorite marketing strategy because your referral sources will be in contact with people who are ready to purchase. You go to the doctor and she recommends that you go to physical therapy. You agree and ask her who she recommends. She provides a couple referrals, you select one, and you go. When a prospective client asks for a referral, you are in a position of filling a need. This is like the house hunters who have narrowed down their target neighborhood, received mortgage approval, found a real estate agent, and would like to move within two months, versus the people who attended an open house because they drove by, saw a sign, and were curious what the house looked like on the inside.

How can you help your referral providers find the right clients for you? One of the most important things you can do is to paint a crystal clear picture of the types of clients you help. This way you will be the person who comes to mind when they have that type of client or patient. When you meet with referral sources, say things like:

- "My clients are new technology businesses who need to set themselves apart with their visual brand."
- "People hire me to help them during the critical first month that their new dog is home, to ensure the dog is well trained and never aggressive with their young children."

- "The children I work with are bright and may have compensated for their attention or learning difficulty for some time, but as they enter middle school and the work gets harder, they find that they need new learning tools to succeed in school."

Can you see how the picture of the client is painted? Your expertise is also highlighted.

Another thing you will need to do is to say no to referrals that are not your ideal clients. This may be hard because you want new clients, but it is necessary. Saying no defines your target client market, showcases your specialty, and communicates your professional ethics because you do not work with people outside of your expertise. It also ensures that you are providing the best possible service to those who you're most qualified to help and enhances your work satisfaction since you'll be working with only your ideal clients. Earlier we discussed the importance of having a referral database. You can then refer your referral source to one of these professionals. Do not be afraid that they will not come back to you again in the future—they will, with your ideal client.

If you happen to get a new client and can tell you are not the best one to help her, refer out immediately. Do not worry that you are losing a client; referring out will actually help you grow your business. In gardening, it is necessary to "deadhead" plants. This means that you remove the flowers that are dead. It helps the plant to grow and flower much better. Similarly, you need to remove any clients who drain you or for whom you are not the best fit. They will be better served elsewhere, and you and your business will flourish.

Why People Buy

ACTION STEPS

1. **Complete this sentence: "Clients hire me to . . ."** This will help you get crystal clear on the needs of your clients and the benefits of your services.

2. **Say this sentence or some variation—"My clients are . . ."**—when describing what you do to potential referral partners.

3. **Package your services into six or fewer programs.** Even if you can't put a specific fee or time limit to your programs, you can create names for the programs.

4. **Avoid using "cost" or "price."** These words have a negative connotation. If you're able to package your services into programs, you can say: "The investment for the Shave 20 Percent or More off Your Overhead Expenses program is $2,500." If you charge by the hour, say hourly fee rather than cost or price.

5. **Refer out.** Practice saying no to referrals who are not your ideal clients. Refer out new clients who you are not best equipped to help, and facilitate the transition to their new service provider. Call them to be sure the new connection is working out or to provide additional referrals or resources that they may need.

6. **Tell people what you'd like them to do.** Make your call to action specific and actionable. A study cited in *Twitter Power 2.0* by Joel Comm found that the best way to influence people to take action to follow you on Twitter is with the statement: "Follow me on twitter here." Lowercase *twitter* and *here* showed the best clickthrough when compared with *Twitter* and *Here*. Even better was to include "you should" at the beginning so it reads "You should follow me on twitter here." Personally, I'm not crazy about the sound of it with "you should," but I can see why it works: because it's curiosity inducing. You want to check out the profile to see why you should follow.

No Choice or a Handful of Choices?

As we've discussed, choice can be a great thing. It empowers people with the sense that they can select the best option for themselves. It can also be a bad thing when people are presented with too many options and decide not to buy. We know that most of the research in which choice proved to be a good thing used six of fewer choices. But should you offer no choice and just one option, or a few, or six? Let's explore the factors to consider.

One versus several

Kathleen, the speaker described at the beginning of this chapter, provided three choices in her call to action. I said that was too many, whereas I provided examples of a professional's program offerings with three or more options. I offer six coaching programs myself. Why?

Well, first of all, Kathleen was offering a "call to action." This is different than offering different programs. Here are some examples of a call to action:

- The one thing that you want people to do when they visit your Web site (for example, sign up for your mailing list).
- The one thing that you want people to do after they hear you speak.
- The one thing that you want people to do when they view your new video.
- The one thing that you want people to do when they read your article.

See what's the same about all of these: "the *one* thing" you want someone to *do*. When your goal is to influence someone to do something right away, it is ideal to not include a choice. Imagine that I said to my son, "Can you go get me my cell phone or go get me the dog's leash or go get your jacket?" He would just stand there and look at me. If I were calling him to action right in that moment, I would want to focus on just one thing—the cell phone or the dog leash or the jacket. So, if you're motivating someone to do one thing at the moment, it is best to go with one call to action.

Seconds versus minutes

Another factor to consider is how long someone has to make a decision or take action. If someone visits your Web site, you have very little time to incite them to take action before they leave your site. If someone sees a post on your Facebook wall, you have very little time for them to think of a response to post on your wall before they move on to something else. If, however, someone is meeting with you in your office or talking with you by phone and you're going over your program options with them, you have more time. Time is closely connected to guidance. If they are on their own, they are likely to be faster and rush to a decision than if they are interacting with you directly.

Obvious versus unclear differences

If the differences between options are unclear, even two options can be too many. The other day I received a piece of marketing from two local real estate agents. It was a pretty good piece of marketing because they added value, as we discussed in Chapter 7, by providing the prices for which houses in my neighborhood recently sold along with information about the trends in mortgages and home sales in my area. Even though I wasn't ready to sell my house, their marketing was interesting to me, and I would remain open to future materials from them.

The mistake they made: the flyer came from two agents. I didn't know if they were partners or how it worked. They had different cell phone numbers. If I wanted to call, I wouldn't know who to call. The flyer coming from two people prevented the dialogue-based communication style I recommend, in which it feels like someone is speaking directly with you. In this case, I didn't know who I was speaking with. (They also failed to use "I" or "we," which limited the personal connection.) If someone can't discern between two people, in a situation like this, she will usually choose either the first or the one who is most similar to herself. When people must make a choice between two similar options, they may choose none at all. If the differences between choices are hard to detect and are not obvious, include fewer or no choices.

When the choices are among related but different categories, it is fine to have more choices as well. For example, my Web design company, One Lily, has a beautiful services page that clearly features the services: logo design, Web design, blog design, marketing materials, Web maintenance, domain registration. Most people know whether they are looking for a logo versus a Web site, for example, so having several types of services is no problem. Part of the reason that the six service offerings work so well is because of how nicely they are presented visually, which leads to the next point. . . .

Verbal versus visual

Another consideration is whether you will present your information verbally or visually and if it's something that people will have to refer to later. People differ in the ways in which they process information—some people do well with hearing and remembering information whereas others do better with information in writing. The more choices people need to compare, the more they will need to see the options in writing. It is still a good idea to keep the choices limited, but you can include more when you present them through writing or pictures (visual) rather than just saying them (verbal).

The choices need to clearly stand out from each other as well as from additional information (such as a description for each choice). The challenge is to do this artfully without everything becoming too busy. I typically recommend varying one aspect, such as the color for each option. There can be a different logo for each option if you're able to achieve this with brand consistency and without getting too busy. Remember the apples to oranges idea. If I handed you six Red Delicious apples and asked which you wanted, you might have a hard time selecting. If, however, I handed you a Red Delicious apple, a Granny Smith apple, an orange, a banana, and a kiwi, you'd have an easier time selecting. You know what you want and could quickly recognize it. This goes along with the previous point about differences as well—if the items are very different, you may even be able to get away with saying rather than showing the options. If I asked you if you want an apple, pear, orange, banana, or kiwi, you could probably make a choice fairly quickly even without seeing them (and five is a lot of options to choose from). These fruits are all quite simple in appearance—that is how you would want your different visual elements to be as well: different from each other in a simple way.

No Choice or a Handful of Choices?

ACTION STEPS

1. **Ask yourself, "What is the one thing I want someone to do?"** for your various marketing activities. If you can't come up with one thing, or you come up with several things, revise your marketing communications to have one primary call to action.

2. **Do the scan test.** Most people scan materials rather than read them. Scan through your materials and see if in just a couple of seconds you can pick out the main options. If you can't, revise the visual presentation to be sure that each is distinct.

3. **Do the memory test.** After scanning your materials, ask yourself if you can remember the different options. If not, you have too many. People can typically remember around six or seven pieces of information (this may be why six emerged in research as a good limited number of options to give). If you have too many, condense and simplify the options.

4. **Package options for clients.** If you're in a field in which your client can choose from unlimited options (such as interior design or real estate), package options for them. An interior designer can create three design motifs from which the client can choose. A real estate agent can create three packages of houses (for example, midcentury modern ranches, new construction, and two-story colonials) to help clients narrow down their taste preferences. Remember that your job is to help clients choose; that's why they hire you. To be undecided is uncomfortable. To decide feels good.

Which Option Will People Choose?

Your clients have options. If you were the only option, you wouldn't need this book—everyone would choose you. Instead, there are probably many options (your "competitors," in traditional marketing lingo) from whom clients can choose. They need to choose between you versus other service providers. They may also need to choose among your products or services. What are they likely to do?

With more options, people go for the more simple

We've discussed how presenting too many options prevented people from making a jam purchase. Too many choices has also been shown to prevent people from taking out a loan and enrolling in a 401(k) plan. One study showed that when 401(k) plans had five funds, 72 percent of people participated, but when plans had 35 funds, participation dropped to 67.5 percent, and with 56 funds, participation went down to 61 percent. For each additional 10 funds, participation decreased by about 2 percent. Extensive choice decreases participation or purchase. But what happens when people are faced with a number of options and do make a decision? What option do they choose?

Contextual inference theory states that people select the simpler option when they are presented with numerous options. Sheena S. Iyengar of Columbia University's Graduate School of Business and Emir Kamenica of the University of Chicago's Graduate School of Business set out to further explore this concept. They conducted three studies, which are published in the article "Choice Overload and Simplicity Seeking." The first study looked at the role of risk and choice. People gambled on either 11 or 3 coin tosses. People would get $4.50 for heads and $7.75 for tails. In each group (11 or 3), 1 toss was a sure thing, where people would automatically get $5. In the 11 tosses, 10 were chance and 1 was a certain $5; in the 3 toss, 2 were chance and 1 was a certain $5. Results were striking: People were more likely to choose the sure bet ($5) in the 11 toss group than in the 3 toss group. People are less accepting of risk when there are more options. In this experiment, the least risky option was also the simplest, so the researchers conducted a second study to discover whether the simplicity or the least risky piece factor was more important.

In the second study, participants received a monetary amount for the number of dots on the die (1–6), so there would be 6 potential outcomes for each toss. For the 11 toss group, 10 tosses resulted in payouts ranging from $0 to $10, and one toss was risky—either $0 or $10. In the 3 toss group, 2 tosses received the range of payouts, and 1 was the risky $0 or $10. So the simpler gamble was also the more risky gamble. Results showed that people chose the simple (and more risky) gamble more often in the 11 choice set (57 percent of the time) than in the 3 choice set (just 16 percent of time), showing that with more choices, people choose the simplest option.

In the third study, the researchers looked at people's behavior in the real world. They examined employees' allocation of assets into their 401(k) plans by reviewing data provided by the Vanguard Center for Retirement Research, including 639 defined contribution (DC) pension plans with 588,926 employees ranging in income from $10,000 to $1,000,000. Employers in 538 of these plans offered some sort of contribution matching. Funds per plan averaged 11, with 90 percent of plans having 6–25 fund options. The researchers looked at how people invested in a mix of seven different types: money market, bond, balanced, active stock, indexed stock, company stock, and other funds. They found that as the number of funds increased, people were more likely to contribute to money market or bond funds (seen by consumers as more simple and less risky). For every additional 10 funds, people allocated on average 3.28 percent more to money market and bond funds at the expense of equity funds. These results tell us that in the real world, just as in laboratory experiments, more choices tend to lead to people selecting the simpler options.

What does this mean for you? First, consider the competition in your field. It is likely that your clients have several other service providers from whom to choose. If this is the case, the simpler your services and your message to them, the more likely they are to choose you. Second, if you offer several products and services, people may be more likely to select the simplest one.

With more options, people go for (and stick with) the ideal

Alexander Chernev gave people an option of chocolates from either a set of 4 or a set of 16. He looked at whether someone had an "ideal point" of reference (a predetermined notion of ideal attributes). He found that people choosing from the 16 chocolates were more satisfied and less likely to switch chocolates when given the option if they had an ideal point of reference in their minds. The ideal point may be a way for people to mentally simplify complex information and decisions.

He replicated the study by offering participants a choice of four products (a Caribbean vacation, a couch, a refrigerator, and a computer case). Findings were consistent with the prior study, showing that people tended to be less satisfied with their decision when selecting from a large group unless they had an ideal point of reference in mind. When they had ideal attributes, they were more confident and satisfied with their decisions.

Applying this idea in a service context, if decisions made from a larger assortment of choices can lead to weaker preferences, decisions from a lot of choices could lead to a client's weaker commitment to staying with you, the service provider. If, however, the client had an ideal point of reference and you were a close fit, the client would be more likely to be satisfied with the decision to stay with you and not make a switch. You can help clients see their ideal attributes (that hopefully you fill and, if not, you can make a referral) by asking them what they are or providing a list from which to choose. If you know your clients' ideal attributes (fast, thoughtful, thorough, et cetera) in a service provider and can use those in your marketing, they will see how you match their ideal reference point.

Be wary of trade-offs and the "attraction effect"

When buyers are faced with a trade-off between two options, they tend to get stuck. For example, a trade-off may be that someone needs a new hairdresser for both cut and color and they are trying to decide between someone who is great with color but not with cutting and someone who is great with cutting and not with color. If a third option is introduced who is good (but not great) on a particular dimension, people are more likely to purchase the option that is great on that dimension. If a third hairdresser is good with color but poor with cutting, people will hire the hairdresser who's great with color. It's funny because the original two options didn't change, but the first suddenly seems more attractive when the third is introduced. Psychologists call this the "attraction effect" and theorize that it comes about to lessen someone's difficulty making a trade-off decision.

Research scientists William Hedgcock and Akshay R. Rao used functional magnetic resonance image (fMRI) scanning to study people's brain activity as they were engaged in a task in which they needed to choose between trade-offs. They found that when people had to make a choice that did not involve a trade-off (i.e., there was a clearly superior option), they had lower activation in brain areas responsible for negative emotion. When a third choice was introduced to employ the attraction effect, negative emotions were also less likely. Thus, our brains don't like trade-offs, and the attraction effect may exist to reduce the negative emotion that comes along with having to make a trade-off decision.

We learn a few things from this "attraction effect." First, do not offer two things that can be seen as a trade-off because people will typically select neither. Second, try to not be compared with another person or business when a trade-off may occur in your client's mind. Third, introduce a third option that is a little lower on one dimension to influence people to select the option higher in that dimension.

Do people tend to select the middle option?

As you see from the attraction effect previously described, if you have three choices—two trade-off options and one that is good but inferior on a dimension—people will select the option that is superior on that particular dimension. In this case, the order in which you present options is unlikely to be as important. As a general rule, however, people tend to select the middle option when all else is equal or when they don't have enough information available to make an informed decision. Let's say that you're a coach and you offer three coaching programs: the first is a month, the second is three months, and the third is six months. In this scenario, people are most likely to select the middle program. Question what the purpose is of offering three programs. You could simply offer a three-month program that people could extend if they were experiencing benefit. If, on the other hand, people tend to do a month or two of coaching, offering three options including a longer one may influence people to select the middle (three-month) program.

Are people even aware of their choice process?

Numerous studies show that many of the factors that influence our decision making are outside of our conscious awareness. Things such as memories, perception, context or frame of reference, and mood can be out of our conscious awareness.

One interesting study found that the way that information is given impacts behavior, even if the information is presented in the form of a hypothetical question. The researchers presented negative information about a political candidate as fact, and presented others with negative information about the candidate as a hypothetical ("If you learned that Bob Clark had been indicted for fraud, would your opinion of him improve or worsen?"). They measured people's voting behaviors and found that people who were presented with either information as fact or as a hypothetical question both decreased voting for Bob Clark. In another experiment, they presented positive information: "If strong evidence emerges from scientific studies suggesting that cakes, pastries, etc. are not nearly as bad for your health as they have often been portrayed to be, and may have some major health benefits, what would happen to your consumption of these items?" They later measured how much people chose chocolate cake versus fruit salad, and found that people who had been given this hypothetical question were more likely to choose chocolate cake than fruit salad. Therefore, information presented as a hypothetical had a significant impact on people's choices—even to the same extent that information presented as fact did. They also found that people were not consciously aware of the impact of the hypothetical question.

Another interesting finding is that when researchers asked participants to think more about the hypothetical question (which we would expect would help them see how it might influence their behavior and enable them to correct the bias), their behavior actually showed *more* bias based on the hypothetical question. If your company uses focus groups or other such methods of marketing research in which you ask people hypothetical questions, be wary of the results and how likely they are to predict future behavior. When participants' thought processes are unconsciously contaminated by hypothetical scenarios, their responses may be biases and not predictive of how other people will actually evaluate or purchase products.

No matter what, make it easy to choose you

The other day, I went online to buy a gift certificate for a restaurant. They didn't have an online purchase form, so I called. The woman who answered the phone told me that I had to download a form online, print it, fill it out with my credit card information, and send it in by fax or scan. Wow, that's a lot of steps to purchase something. If it weren't a gift for my sister, I never would have gone through all of that. The smallest things can make a big difference in whether or not people take action to connect with, buy from, refer to, or hire you.

The most important thing that you can do is to make things easy for people. If someone's about to spend money, the last thing she wants is for it to be a pain to do so. Even if you're asking someone to do something that doesn't involve spending money, make it ridiculously easy for them. For example, I am active on the social networking community LinkedIn. I often get long e-mails from people asking to connect and telling me all about themselves. As you now know, short is better than long, so keep your e-mails succinct and to the point. Additionally, if you're asking someone to do something, such as connect, make it easy. Send the connection request. When someone doesn't do this, I need to go ahead and send them a request. Sure, this isn't a big deal, it just takes a minute, but it's one of those small things that makes a big difference.

Which Option Will People Choose?

ACTION STEPS

1. **Give yourself the "the . . ." test.** You are *the* what? (For instance, I'm *the* marketing psychologist for service businesses.) If you find yourself saying "and" or speaking a run-on sentence, you are unlikely to stand out as the most simple and clear option. This is especially important in a saturated field. Revise your branding and your marketing message to have one clear benefit. Put your stake in the ground to stand for one thing.

2. **Avoid two choices that could include a trade-off.** Instead, package your programs into three options and know that if one of them is slightly less desirable on a given trait, the program that is stronger on that trait (even though weaker in others) is likely to emerge as the most selected option.

3. **Be aware of hypothetical questions.** You could significantly influence someone's behavior by asking a hypothetical question.

4. **Create a program that is a bit longer than what people naturally do.** Let's say that you find that people typically end enrollment in your services after five months. Create a six-month program to extend their enrollment and enhance the benefits of your services.

5. **Send your connection requests** rather than asking someone to send a request to you. Consider people's time even if it's just a matter of seconds because convenience is appreciated and reciprocated.

We're almost at the end of our journey into the psychology of how people think, build relationships, and buy. Just one final piece: how do people ultimately decide (to hire you)?

Chapter 12

Influence Action—
People Decide in the Opposite Way
of What You'd Think

With all its cleverness, decision theory is somewhat crippled
emotionally, and thus detached from the emotional and visceral
richness of life.

—GEORGE LOWENSTEIN

YOU'VE ALREADY DONE the work to make it rain with clients, clients, and
more clients. You've found the right people. You've captured attention
and emotion. You've established yourself as a credible expert in your field.
You've made yourself memorable and furthered relationships by following
up and adding value. You've built a sense of community through stimulating conversations, and you've shown people how you help others like
them. You've given and activated the law of reciprocity. You've even presented people with a singular message and call to action. So, what's left?
Not much—they just need to decide to hire you. The traditional view
of decision making is that people make a pros and cons list and go with

whatever choice is most compelling. This is not necessarily true. In this chapter, we'll explore how people actually make decisions and the things you should do (and not do) to help them decide to hire *you*.

What Happens When Heart and Mind Are in Conflict?

Susan is a 30-year-old regional manager for a major retailer. She decided that she needed assistance with managing her finances. A true self-starter, Susan had been working since the age of 16, when she got her first job in a grocery store. Growing up in a working-class family, she understood the value of hard work and saving money. She waited tables to pay her way through college and got a job as a retail store assistant manager immediately after college. She quickly worked her way up, and by the time she was 29, she was a regional manager for all of the East Coast.

When Susan was 27, she unexpectedly became pregnant and had a healthy baby girl. She had an on-again, off-again relationship with the father of her child but was thrilled to be a mother. Susan ended up leaving her boyfriend. Her daughter's father was negligent with paying child support, so Susan took him to court and racked up hefty legal bills. Despite this, she was an excellent saver and was ready to learn more about investing her savings by hiring a financial planner.

Susan decided to meet with two financial planners and select one. Because of her history with money and her determination to save for her daughter's education, the decision of who to hire was an important and complex one. She knew that she would need to trust the advisor but beyond that wasn't sure how she would decide.

Both financial planners were middle-aged men from midsized financial services firms. The first, Bill, was dressed professionally in a navy blue suit, white shirt, and red "power" tie. He had an impressive background, including degrees from Ivy League institutions and substantial wealth management experience. Bill was very detail oriented and believed in giving his clients all of the information they needed to make an informed decision. As such, he went through several models of financial planning, extensive decision-making tools, statistics from past client experiences, and details of his own background, including his education, training, and so on.

The second advisor who Susan met with was named Steve. Steve had a more casual style than Bill. He didn't have the prestigious background that Bill had and didn't go much into his background at all. Instead he asked Susan questions, shared a few key pieces of information for her to consider, and answered her questions. She liked Steve and felt comfortable with him.

Who did Susan choose?

Susan was stumped. She went over all the facts (most of which were provided by Bill) for hours. She worried about making the wrong decision. When she wrote a pros and cons list, Bill emerged as the best choice, so she decided on Bill.

Just as she was about to call Bill to get started, however, she noticed an uneasy feeling in her stomach. She couldn't shake the idea that she liked Steve and wanted to hire him even though the data seemed to point to the contrary. Because she'd learned over time to trust her instincts, she decided to go with her gut and hire Steve. Susan and Steve ended up working very well together, and she could not have been more pleased with her decision.

Going with the heart leads to happiness

Susan made an excellent decision—and one that seemed to fly in the face of reason. When faced with an important and complicated decision, wouldn't she have been better off to weigh all of her options in detail? Wasn't Bill better, showing up so well prepared and giving her all of the information to consider?

Actually, no.

Research on decision making tells us that people are happier with decisions when they go with their emotions. This seems strange because we've learned to make rational decisions and make pros and cons lists or conduct cost-benefit analyses.

Benjamin Franklin said of his process for making decisions:

My way is to divide half a sheet of paper by a line into two columns, writing over the one Pro, and over the other Con. Then, during three or four days' consideration, I put down under the different heads short hints of the different motives, that at different times occur to me, for or against each measure . . . I find at length where the balance lies; and if, after a day or two of further consideration, nothing new that is of importance occurs on either side, I come to a determination accordingly . . . When each [reason] is thus considered, separately and comparatively, and the whole lies before me, I think I can judge better, and am less likely to make a rash step.

Have you done something like this yourself?

We all have, and it seems to help. Benjamin Franklin was a pretty smart guy, and his approach is consistent with what has been taught for years about how to make decisions—that we should objectively weigh all of the variables.

After all, the ability to problem-solve and think through all of the options is a uniquely human characteristic. Our prefrontal cortex (the part of the top and front of the brain behind our foreheads) is the most evolved part of the brain and allows us to consider options, weigh contingencies, plan for the future, and so on. Shouldn't we use it? And shouldn't we give our clients extensive information so they can use their prefrontal cortexes? Not necessarily.

Too much analysis leads to unhappiness

Researchers Timothy D. Wilson and Jonathan W. Schooler were curious if overanalysis was linked with unhappiness. So they investigated real-life choices of college students about what course to take the following semester. The students were give in-depth information about the psychology courses being offered and were asked to think about how all of the different variables impacted their preferences. For "expert" ratings, the researchers looked at the ratings of students who had already taken the courses. These ratings showed that some courses were rated more favorably while others were rated less favorably. The results showed that the students in the study who were given all of the information and asked to analyze their choices changed the way they rated the courses. Like the jam preferences, they ended up making less optimal choices. The students who reviewed all of the information were more likely to select the courses that were rated less favorably by the experts than those in the control group who did not analyze their reasoning.

In the last chapter, we discussed how people faced with many options of jam ended up not purchasing any. Here is another interesting study about jam and decision making: Timothy Wilson from the University of Virginia and Jonathan Schooler from the University of Pittsburgh and their team purchased five brands of strawberry jam ranked 1, 11, 24, 32, and 44 by *Consumer Reports*. The undergraduate student participants were assigned to one of two groups: a control group where they were just asked to rate their opinions of the jam, and a reason analysis group where they were asked to rate their opinions and then say why they felt that way. After tasting the jam on little spoons and crackers, those in the reason analysis group completed a questionnaire about their reasons for liking the jams. Those in the control group completed no questionnaire or a filler about their major. All were asked to indicate how much they liked the jam on a scale of one (did not like) to nine (liked). The results showed that those in the control group rated jam similarly to the *Consumer Reports* expert ratings. On the other hand, those who were asked to explain their ratings came up with reasons that didn't correspond to the way experts rated the jams.

Those who were asked to think about their reasons changed how they felt about the jams (how much they liked them) because they focused on certain aspects from their analysis that were not important in their initial evaluations. For example, someone may have loved jam number two, but when asked for a rationale, more reasons came to mind for jam number four. Because the ratings of those who had to explain their feelings differed substantially from expert ratings, we can conclude that a rational thought process distorts our views and can lead to less favorable choices. This is similar to how Susan initially liked Steve, but when she weighed all of her options, she started focusing on facts about Bill—such as the name of his college and the fact that he graduated at the top of his class—that were less important in her initial reaction. Because of this analysis, she felt like she should choose Bill, but she probably would have been less happy if she had.

What Happens When Heart and Mind Are in Conflict?

ACTION STEPS

1. **Provide only essential information.** Help your client understand the few most important factors in his or her decision about whether or not to hire you, and focus only on those.

2. **Allow your client to outsource her anxiety.** Let her know that she doesn't have to have it all figured out and be an expert; that is your job. She just needs to decide if she feels comfortable working with you and if she has any important questions to ask you to help make that decision.

3. **Ask great questions.** In the beginning of the book, we discussed how your initial goal in meeting with someone is to develop rapport and establish a relationship. These same skills will help you "close the sale" and enroll new clients. Make it your goal to understand your clients, build rapport, and answer their questions rather than to deliver a bunch of information.

4. **Provide take-away information that does not lend itself to over-analysis.** Avoid extensive use of charts, graphs, data, and other things that someone will feel compelled to sit down with and evaluate in making a decision. Instead provide a simple one-page summary sheet. Include visuals or ways to simplify information and make it easier to digest.

5. **Be careful if you ask your clients why.** You may be tempted to ask your client why he hired you. Your thinking is on track because you want to gain data to help with your marketing research, but you run the risk of two problems: First, the client may not be honest. We don't feel comfortable giving a "dumb" answer like "I just liked you," so we may focus on details that did not actually influence us. Second, the client may be less happy with his decision, like those in the jam study were. Better to focus on the specific problem that the client stated when he first met you. He hired you because he felt that you'd be the best person to help him with that specific problem. Remember, it isn't so much about *you* as how you can help *him*.

Is the Decision to Hire or Buy from You Complex or Simple?

An interesting finding in psychology research is that people make decisions differently if the decision is a simple one versus a complex one.

When less is best

A psychologist at The University of Amsterdam named Ap Dijksterhuis observed people shopping for furniture at IKEA. Furniture shopping can involve complex decisions because there are so many variables to consider. Similar to the findings of the ham study, Dijksterhuis found that when people spent a longer amount of time analyzing their decisions, they became less happy with their decisions. The shoppers who didn't spend much time thinking and just went with their gut reactions were the most happy.

When we are faced with making a complicated decision, the prefrontal cortex part of our brain comes into play. This part of our brain wants to analyze everything, problem-solve, rationalize, and plan for the future. Our prefrontal cortexes can get in the way of good decisions.

If you're a pros and cons list type of person and you're having a hard time believing all of this, you're right on some level. While it is true that going with gut reactions is often ideal, this is not always the case.

When more is called for

Dijksterhuis ran another study in which he observed people who had to make a decision about a less complex purchase: cooking accessories, such as can openers and vegetable peelers. In these relatively simple purchases, he found that the people who spent a brief period of time analyzing their options were happier in the long run than those who went with their gut and made an impulse buy.

Why is this the case?

With simple decisions, the options are limited. We can fairly quickly review the most important factors such as price, feel or ergonomic quality, durability, and appearance. It seems that there is a fine line in what qualifies something as simple (a consumer product) versus more complicated (strawberry jam, which has several dimensions including chunkiness, color, fruitiness, tartness, spreadability, sweetness, healthfulness, and so on).

Why is it better to analyze some things than others?

Perhaps this relates to the number of variables we can process at once in our working memory, as we discussed in Chapter 5. The data showed that if the variables are quite simple, it can be around five to seven, but if the variables are about relationships, three is the maximum number. Beyond that, it just becomes too taxing on our minds. Why would we want to work so hard so we can pay someone our money?

When we're faced with complicated decisions and too much information, we feel stupid when we can't figure it out. Feeling stupid is among our worst fears—even if we just feel stupid in front of ourselves. We will jump to deciding "no" rather than deal with the discomfort of not knowing and trying to figure it out. Research by Rebecca Hamilton and Debora Viana Thompson suggests that when evaluating a single product, helping people to focus on the process facilitates their choosing the more viable alternative. One way to do this is to help them imagine using the product.

On the other hand, when someone is faced with evaluating multiple offerings, a focus on the process in addition to the outcome is detrimental. In one study, students were given two scenarios about different apartments from which to choose. One was closer to campus and one was larger. When asked to think about the process (living there each day) versus the outcome (benefits), students in the process-condition rated the task as more difficult, were less confident in and committed to their decisions, and were more willing to delay making a choice.

To determine which offerings were complex and which were simple, one of my clients created an inventory of all the products and services sold in his business and listed out the elements of each. For the simple products, he provided clients and customers with brief checklists of product characteristics. He included images of people using the product. For the complex products, he kept the information simple to allow clients to go with their instincts or referral recommendations, and he focused his marketing on the results rather than the process.

Is the Decision to Hire or Buy from You Complex or Simple?

ACTION STEPS

1. **When it's you versus another, focus on the outcome over process.** When people are deciding between alternatives, they find it frustrating to evaluate processes and easier to imagine specific outcomes. They also are more likely to take action when they imagine outcomes.

2. **If it's just you under consideration, discuss process.** If you have reason to believe they are not selecting among alternatives (it's you or no one), a process focus is helpful.

3. **Provide more information for simpler decisions.** Let's say that you sell an information product such as a video. Include three to five crucial pieces of information to consider for this product.

4. **Present information graphically.** Especially if you're comparing your products to one another or your products to other products, include the information in a graph or table, which serves as an aid to help people process the information. This is recommended for selling products or one-time events but not for ongoing relationship services, which are considered more complex.

Strike While the Iron's Hot (or Not)

There is some truth to the sales advice that you need to strike while the iron's hot (i.e., get someone to make a decision right away), but research suggests that the reason may be the over-analysis that occurs when people think about a decision, not the time that lapses.

If someone does not continue to think about the choices but instead allows the options to simmer on the back-burner, allowing their unconscious mind to process the information, they tend to be happy with their choice.

Thinking about hiring you isn't good

When people tell you, "I'll think about it," you know that is not a good thing—not just because they aren't committed to hiring you right away but because over-thinking leads to less optimal decisions. It can also be that they realize that their gut is saying no but they don't want to say no, so "I'll think about it" is a way to let you down easy. When this happens, ask yourself if you may have focused on the less relevant things (giving out a lot of information) versus the more relevant things (building trust, rapport, and understanding their needs) and what you can do differently the next time. Or perhaps their intuition was leading them in the right direction and they are not your ideal clients.

A consultant, Abigail, who came to me for coaching told me that she was doing very well with her marketing but for some reason after she spoke with her prospective clients, the initial calls almost always ended with the prospective client saying, "Thanks so much, I'll think about it and get back to you soon." In analyzing these initial conversations, I realized that she was talking clients out of hiring her! Here's how.

You had them at hello

When you've used the ideas we've discussed thus far, you won't need to sell. People come to you with a positive feeling. They know, like, and trust you. They realize that you're the go-to expert to help them. When you start to "sell," you run the risk of talking them out of these things. That is precisely what Abigail did. She got nervous about needing to "sell" and "close the deal." As a result, she rambled and tried to give people a lot of information so they would see that she was a great choice for them. Hiring Abigail was a complex decision, so all of this information was not a good idea. Abigail was also concerned about coming across as pushy or as rushing people, so she booked an hour for this initial call. Having that hour made her feel pressured to fill up the time. Giving away an hour of her time also reduced the perception of her value in the minds of her potential clients.

Abigail had done the previous steps that we've discussed very well, so when her clients came to her, they had already marinated with the information and were ready to hire her. She needed to keep it simple and "strike while the iron's hot." I suggested that she do this by scheduling an hour long *paid* consultation, the first 15 minutes of which would be free. Her clients did not need to pay until the end of the initial meeting. Or, if they paid up front, they could receive a refund if they did not get value, which thus far has never happened. If in the first 15 minutes Abigail realized she was not a great match to help a potential client, she provided a referral and there was no charge. If in the first 15 minutes she and the client realized that they were a good match, they jumped right into the consultation and the client was billed for 45 minutes. Clients ended the initial consult feeling great about the services and feeling as though they got 15 minutes for free. And Abigail ended the first session with a new client or a great feeling that she provided an excellent referral. This changed Abigail's mind-set and the mind-set of her new clients. The use of time was completely different, people received a great deal of value from this initial meeting, and she went from hearing "Thank you, I'll think about it" to "Thank you, when can you meet again?"

Some options to consider for your initial consultation include:

- **A free initial consult with the condition that a decision one way or another is made at the end.** If you offer free initial meetings, you can let people know that in your experiences, client relationships work out best when clients go with their gut reaction. There tends to be a chemistry or not, just like in dating, and so you offer a free consult in which people can decide to begin working together or not, in which case you'll provide a referral if there's someone who's a better match.
- **A free initial consult plus a follow-up call.** If the option above doesn't work in your line of work, you can schedule a follow-up call or e-mail (a call is better) within a few days of the initial meeting so people don't overanalyze their options. You can also offer to have people e-mail you questions. You can say that you'll block time in your schedule (within a couple days) to respond to any questions they've thought of.

- **A paid initial consult.** Make your initial consultations paid, and be sure the client receives excellent value. This is like ordering an appetizer in a restaurant—it isn't free, but you tend to want more.

Regardless of how you conduct your initial consultation, it is a good idea to put a time limit to it, such as 20 minutes.

How focused are they?

People decide differently when they have other things on their minds. Consider this study: Baba Shiv and Alexander Fedorikhin gave people numbers to memorize as they made their way to another room where they would repeat the numbers. Some people were asked to memorize a seven-digit number, a mentally challenging task, while others were asked to memorize a two-digit number, a task that did not require ongoing mental effort. On the way to the next room, they were stopped and presented with a piece of chocolate cake or a fruit salad and asked which they would like. Of the people who had been given seven numbers to memorize, 63 percent of people chose cake. Of the people who had been given two numbers, only 41 percent chose cake. These results suggest that when our mental processing resources are taxed (by thinking about something else), we tend to go with our emotions. When our processing resources are not taxed, we tend to focus more on the rational benefits (such as how fruit salad is healthier), and we make different choices.

Are your services more like chocolate cake (whereby an emotional decision would lead to clients enrolling) or more like fruit salad (whereby a bit of thought would lead to clients enrolling)? If your services are like chocolate cake, clients will not be unduly influenced if they're multitasking or have a lot on their minds. If, on the other hand, you're more like fruit salad, ensure that clients are not distracted during your initial meeting. Do not keep them waiting—you know what happens when we are kept waiting: the mental checklists of all the things we need to do take over. Ensure that your office is free from noise, clutter, and other external distractions. If you meet by phone, be sure that the line is crystal clear and that you don't have background noise. Engage the client in discussion early on so they are not thinking of other things while you present information to them.

Understand the law of psychological reactance

This is one of the fundamental rules of relationships: when we feel pushed, we tend to pull back. Now that you know that overthinking decisions is bad, you may be tempted to push prospective clients into making quick decisions. Avoid the temptation to do this because if people feel pushed, they will pull in the other direction.

You can build quick decisions into your process as Abigail did, or ask people when they will have a decision if you do so in a nonpressure way. As we've discussed, the most important aspect of communication is nonverbal—*how* you say something, including your tone of voice, speed of voice, and body language, rather than *what* you say. You can say something like, "When would you want to get started?" or "When do you plan to make a decision?" in a way that people feel supported rather than pressured.

Do not try to use reverse psychology or dishonest tactics such as telling people that you are booked for months so they better make an appointment now (unless, of course, it is true that you are booked for months). These strategies backfire. You won't feel good about stretching the truth, and people can tell that they are being manipulated. They may also think that if you're so busy, you won't have time for them or do a good job with them. Instead, you can make a rule for yourself and state it to your prospective clients. For example, "I take on three new clients per month. Are you interested in beginning in September?" It is also fine to help clients see how you need to manage your schedule and so you need to know if they are going to begin in a certain time frame. Simply present it as a human being, just like you are making lunch plans with a friend, rather than as a salesperson trying to "close the deal."

Know about them to heat up the iron

If there's one take-away message I want to be sure that you get from this book, it's that it's not about you—it's about your client. People don't care as much about *you* as how *you can help them*. My clients love this idea because it really takes the pressure off of them. You don't have to sell yourself. You don't have to push your services. You simply have to learn about your potential client and together determine whether you're the best person to help them. This shift in mind-set is huge because it helps you to be more present and more yourself in your initial meetings. Instead of listening for how to sell yourself to them, you'll listen to their needs, their emotions, and their goals. Instead of asking yourself, "How can I show them how I can help them?" or "How can I explain my qualifications?" you'll ask yourself, "What do they really need?" and "Am I the best person to help them reach that goal?" This process positions you as partners in the decision-making journey rather than you as a salesperson and them as customers or, more dramatically (as it sometimes feels to clients), you as a hunter and them as the prey.

If your clients are businesses or other professionals, give yourself a head start by scheduling time to learn about your potential client before your initial meeting. Don't just read the home page of their Web site—instead take twenty minutes and really dig in to discover as much as you can. This also holds true for organizations that you will speak in front of and referral partners who you will meet with. It sounds basic, but you would be shocked at how many people don't do it or do it in a haphazard rushed way five minutes before an initial meeting.

You may have heard that when people interview applicants for a job, they determine the quality of the applicant by the quality of the questions they ask. You will ask great questions if you have great background information. If you can't find it online, ask people to share it; they will be happy to. And they will be happy to discover that you already know about their background so you can hit the ground running.

Strike while the Iron's Hot (or Not)

ACTION STEPS

1. **Don't talk too much—you've already done everything.** When people are "well qualified" and come to you interested in your services,

do not give too much information or sell yourself. Instead, engage in a dialogue and allow the client to ask questions.

2. **Shift your posture to shift your tone.** Keep yourself from getting nervous and adopting a pressured, salesy tone of voice by keeping your posture open, confident, and relaxed. If you tend to get too fast and pressured on the phone, sit back and put your legs up. If you tend to get insecure, stand up tall with your legs hip-width apart to gain a sense of power and confidence.

3. **Ask when they intend to make a decision.** Don't give a deadline because that feels like pressure; simply ask them what their time line is for making a decision.

4. **Help clients decide.** If you feel that you can be of unbiased assistance in helping people understand the differences between your offerings and others, help them. Remember that you're the expert in your field and your client isn't. For example, if you're a Web designer, your client might know that you do custom WordPress sites while the other person they're considering does HTML, but the client might not really know what this means. When you explain differences, boil it down to the most simple explanation. Be objective and think of the prospective client as a friend or family member, helping her to see that someone else is a better fit than you, if this is the case. You will work with your ideal clients, and you'll have good marketing karma in the future.

5. **Google people, businesses, or organizations before you meet.** If you have a few weeks or months, you can also set up a Google Alert for their name, company, or association so you'll find out about their recent happenings.

6. **Show your enthusiasm.** Don't hesitate to let clients know how interested you are in working with them. Be specific about why you're interested in them. You don't want them to think you say that to everyone. Think of what it feels like when you're a client or patient—you want to know that your professional service provider likes you, is well qualified and dedicated to helping you, and is excited to work with you.

Well, we've come to the end of our journey into understanding the psychology of marketing. You now know how to attract attention, deepen connections, and influence action. I hope you've found at least a couple take-aways that you can implement right away. I also hope that you have a new level of confidence and energy around marketing your services and that you have fun connecting with people.

I would love to change our communication from one-way (me writing, you reading) to two-way (us connecting). Please post comments and questions on my blog, *PsychologyofMarketing.com* and on Facebook.com /MarketingPsych. Introduce yourself and join the discussions!

Now put this book down and get ready to serve clients, clients, and more clients!

References

Chapter 1

p. 12 "Recent research by Dr. Sue Johnson, distinguished research professor at Alliant University in San Diego, California ... has shown that couples that last fulfill one another's basic needs for attachment including closeness, security, and connection.": Sue Johnson, *Hold Me Tight: Seven Conversations for a Lifetime of Love*, New York: Little, Brown and Company, 2008.

p. 17 "I love the dialogue that Michael Port describes in *Book Yourself Solid*.": Michael Port, *Book Yourself Solid*, Hoboken, NJ: Wiley, 2010.

p. 18 "A 2011 *Psychology Today* article stated that women prefer sitting directly across from people, whereas men prefer to sit at an angle.": Kaja Perina, "Secrets of Special Agents," *Psychology Today*, Jan/Feb 2011, 56–63, 86.

Chapter 2

p. 22 "In 2007, Massachusetts Institute of Technology researchers Timothy J. Buschman and Earl K. Miller trained monkeys to complete attention tasks on computers while their brain activity was monitored.": Timothy J. Buschman and Earl K. Miller, "Top-Down Versus Bottom-Up Control of Attention in the Prefrontal and Posterior Parietal Cortices," *Science*, 30, 2007, 1860–1862.

p. 23 "A 2004 study of 1,363 print advertisement with 3,600 consumers investigated whether a business's brand, use of pictures, or text best captured attention.": Rik Pieters and Michel Wedel, "Attention Capture and Transfer in Advertising: Brand, Pictorial, and Text-Size Effects," *Journal of Marketing*, 68, No. 2, 2004, 36–50.

p. 24 "A study by Florida State University researchers published as *Can't Take My Eyes off You* confirmed that our attention tends to become glued to people who we find attractive.": Jon K. Maner, Matthew T. Gailliot, D. Aaron Rouby, and Saul L. Miller, "Can't Take My Eyes off You: Attentional Adhesion to Mates and Rivals," *Journal of Personality and Social Psychology*, Psychological Association, 93, No. 3, 2007, 389–401.

p. 24 "Research conducted by Dustin Wood and Claudia Brumbaugh suggests that there tends to be a greater consensus among men than among women about what they view as physically attractive in the opposite sex.": Justin Wood and Claudia C. Brumbaugh, "Using Revealed Mate Preferences to Evaluate Market Force and Differential Preference Explanations for Mate Selection," *Journal of Personality and Social Psychology*, 96, 2009, 1226–1244.

p. 25 "In one study, 200 undergraduate students rated two measures of attraction: how much they would like a stranger and how much they would enjoy working with that person.": Hilda Mayer Buckley, "Attraction Toward a Stranger as a Linear Function of Similarity in Dress," *Family and Consumer Sciences Research Journal*, 12, 1983, 25–34.

p. 28 "One study by professors in Italy showed that varying color, form, and luminance (or brightness) is effective at capturing attention.": Massimo Turatto and Giovanni Galfano, "Color, Form and Luminance Capture Attention in Visual Search," *Vision Research*, 40, No. 13, 2000, 1639–1643.

p. 30 "Across research studies, two factors have emerged as consistently reliable ways to get attention, and a recent study showed that their power remains even when people's attention is engaged elsewhere: The person's name, a smiley face icon[.]": Arien Mack, Zissis Pappas, Michael Silverman, and Robin Gay, "What We See: Inattention and the Capture of Attention by Meaning," *Consciousness and Cognition*, 11, No. 4, 2002, 488–506.

p. 35 "In one study, three patients who had strokes (in the right parietal part of their brain) showed a greater ability to remember faces with strong emotional expressions, including happy or angry, than faces with neutral expressions.": Patrik Vuilleumier and Sophie Schwartz, "Emotional Facial Expressions Capture Attention," *Neurology*, 56, No. 2, 2001, 153–158.

Chapter 3

p. 37 "In a study of advertisements on Dutch television over the course of a decade, researchers found that commercials that viewers rated as less likeable produced less effective results.": Edith G. Smit, Lex van Meurs, and Peter C. Neijens, "Effects of Advertising Likeability: A 10-Year Perspective," *Journal of Advertising Research*, 46, No. 1, 2006, 73–83.

p. 38 "Dr. William McGuire of Yale University has extensively researched what makes people believe or disbelieve a message.": William McGuire, "Inducing Resistance to Persuasion," in *Advances in Experimental Social Psychology*, ed. L Berkowitz, New York: Academic, 1964, 1: 191–229.

p. 38 "In *Primal Leadership*, emotional intelligence researchers Daniel Goleman, Richard E. Boyatzis, and Annie McKee explain how the mood of leaders is contagious.": Daniel Goleman, Richard E. Boyatzis, and Annie McKee, *Primal Leadership*, Boston: Harvard Business School Press, 2004.

p. 43 "But there's another reason: recent research has shown that the sound of a brand can create positive emotions.": Jennifer J. Argo, Monica Popa, and Malcolm C. Smith, "The Sound of Brands," *Journal of Marketing*, 74, No. 4, July 2010, 97–109.

p. 48 "In the book *Marketing Metaphoria*, Harvard Business School professor Gerald Zaltman and coauthor Lindsay Zaltman discuss the power of deep metaphors.": Gerald

Zaltman and Lindsay Zaltman, *Marketing Metaphoria: What Deep Metaphors Reveal about the Minds of Consumers*, Cambridge, MA: Harvard Business Press, 2008.

Chapter 4

p. 54 "In the early 1950s, Yale University researchers Carl Hovland, Irving Janis, and Harold Kelley created a model to explain what makes a message be perceived as credible.": Carl I. Hovland, Irving L. Janis, and Harold H. Kelley, *Communication and Persuasion: Psychological Studies of Opinion Change*, New Haven, CT: Yale University Press, 1953.

p. 54 "More recently, researcher B.J. Fogg expanded the model to include four key types...": B. J. Fogg, "Prominence-Interpretation Theory: Explaining How People Assess Credibility," report from Stanford Persuasive Technology Lab, Stanford University, 2002, http://credibility.stanford.edu/pit.html, accessed February 15, 2011.

p. 55 "In 2007, Maria Mattus of Linköping University, Sweden, set out to determine how Fogg's four types of credibility came into play as students evaluated the credibility of scientific information on the Web.": Maria Mattus, "Finding Credible Information: A Challenge to Students Writing Academic Essays," *Human IT*, 9, No. 2, 2007, 1–28.

p. 55 "According to research by Gitte Lindgaard and her colleagues at Carleton University in Canada, the length of time is almost impossible to conceive—50 milliseconds.": Gitte Lindgaard, Gary Fernandes, Cathy Dudek, and J. Brown, "Attention Web Designers: You Have 50 Milliseconds to Make a Good First Impression," *Behaviour & Information Technology*, 25, 2006, 115–126.

p. 55 "Stanford University's Persuasive Technology Lab, in collaboration with Sliced Bread Design LLC and Consumer Reports WebWatch, set out to discover what aspects of Web sites people deem as credible or not.": B.J. Fogg, Cathy Soohoo, David R. Danielson, Leslie Marable, Julianne Stanford, and Ellen R. Tauber, "How Do Users Evaluate the Credibility of Web Sites? A Study with over 2,500 Participants," proceedings of DUX2003, Designing for User Experiences Conference, 2003.

p. 58 "Read Trust Agents: Using the Web to Build Influence, Improve Reputation, and Earn Trust by Chris Brogan and Julien Smith.": Chris Brogan and Julien Smith, *Trust Agents: Using the Web to Build Influence, Improve Reputation, and Earn Trust*, Hoboken, NJ: Wiley, 2008.

p. 58 "Stanford Persuasive Technology Lab also ran a study on experts' perceptions of credibility.": Ellen R. Tauber, B. J. Fogg, and Leslie Marable, "Experts vs. Online Consumers: A Comparative Credibility Study of Health and Finance Web Sites," published report, 2002, http://www.consumerwebwatch.org/dynamic/web-credibility-reports-experts-vs-online.cfm, accessed March 2, 2011.

p. 62 "Toby Israel, an environmental psychologist and author of *Some Place Like Home: Using Design Psychology to Create Ideal Spaces*, gave The Myers-Briggs personality test to clients.": Toby Israel, *Some Place Like Home: Using Design Psychology to Create Ideal Places*, Princeton, NJ: Design Psychology Press, 2010.

p. 62 "A 2009 study investigated whether personality features (using the "big five" personality domains: extroversion, agreeableness, conscientiousness, neuroticism, and openness) were related to preference for different types of art (including portraiture, abstract art, geometric art, and impressionism).": Tomas Chamorro-Premuzic, Charlotte Burke,

Anne Hsu, and Viren Swami, "Personality Predictors of Artistic Preferences as a Function of the Emotional Valence and Perceived Complexity of Paintings," *Psychology of Aesthetics, Creativity, and the Arts*, 4, No. 4, 2010, 196–204.

p. 62 "Another study found that brightly colored spaces such as red rooms created an excited state in the brain, which paradoxically lowered heart rates.": Rikard Küller, Byron Mikellides, and Jan Janssens, "Color, Arousal, and Performance—A Comparison of Three Experiments," *Color Research & Application*, 34, 2009, 141–152.

p. 64 "Dr. Robert B. Cialdini, founder of Influence at Work and author of the groundbreaking books *Influence: Science & Practice* and *Yes! 50 Scientifically Proven Ways to Be Persuasive…*": Robert B. Cialdini, *Influence: Science and Practice*, 5th ed., Upper Saddle River, NJ: Prentice Hall, 2008, 36.

p. 64 "In 1971, Philip Zimbardo, a professor of psychology at Stanford University, conducted one of the most illuminating social psychology studies in history, the Stanford prison experiment.": Philip G. Zimbardo, "The Stanford Prison Experiment," http://www.prison exp.org/, accessed January 20, 2011.

p. 65 "Neuroscience research shows that people's brains actually respond differently when the person speaking with them is an expert. In one study, when the communicator was an expert, functional magnetic resonance imaging showed activity in the prefrontal and temporal cortices, which involve active processing and elaboration.": Vasily Klucharev, Ale Smidts, and Guillén Fernández, "Brain Mechanisms of Persuasion: How 'Expert Power' Modulates Memory and Attitudes," *Social, Cognitive, and Affective Neuroscience*, 3, 2008, 353–66.

Chapter 5

p. 76: "Australian researchers from the University of Queensland gave people a sentence like the following…": Graeme S. Halford, Rosemary Baker, Julie E. McCredden, and John D. Bain, "How Many Variables Can Humans Process?" *Psychological Science*, 16, No. 1, 2005, 70–76.

p. 77 "Dartmouth College researchers recruited 24 participants ages 18 to 30 and set them up with functional magnetic resonance imaging (fMRI) to measure their brain activity.": W.M. Kelley, C.N. Macrae, C.L. Wyland, S. Caglar, S. Inati, and T.F. Heatherton, "Finding the Self: An Event-Related fMRI Study," *Journal of Cognitive Neuroscience*, 14, No. 5, 2002, 785–794.

p. 77 "Studies have shown that this powerful self-referential effect is reduced if the judgments about others are for those we are closely connected to, such as our family members or good friends.": J. M. Keenan and S. D. Baillet, "Memory for Personally and Socially Significant Events," *Attention and Performance*, ed. Raymond S. Nickerson, Hillsdale, NJ: Erlbaum, 1980, 651–669.

p. 79 "Research on ad placements during the 2006 Super Bowl showed that the first ads were remembered best.": Cong Li, "Primacy Effect or Recency Effect? A Long-Term Memory Test of Super Bowl Commercials," *Journal of Consumer Behaviour*, 9, 2010, 32–44; Howard Eichenbaum, A.P. Yonelinas, and C. Ranganath, "The Medial Temporal Lobe and Recognition Memory," *Annual Review of Neuroscience*, 30, 2007, 123–152.

Chapter 6

p. 88 "The idea put forth by marketing visionary Seth Godin in *Permission Marketing* is that you want to be in touch with people by providing value rather than interruption.": Seth Godin, *Permission Marketing: Turning Strangers into Friends and Friends into Customers*, New York: Simon & Schuster, 1999.

p. 91 "In a 2006 article in the *Harvard Business Review*, Fordham University Professor of Management Robert F. Hurley lays out a trust model based on characteristics of both the truster and the situation or trustee...": Robert F. Hurley, "The Decision to Trust," *Harvard Business Review*, 84, No. 9, 2006, 55.

p. 92 "In 2007, researchers F. David Schoorman, Roger C. Mayer, and James H. Davis reevaluated a seminal model of trust they developed in 1995.": F. David Schoorman, Roger C. Mayer, and James H. Davis, "Editors Forum: An Integrative Model of Organizational Trust: Past, Present, and Future," *The Academy of Management Review*, 32, No. 2, 2007, 344–354.

p. 93 "Researchers Dunn and Schweitzer found that someone's emotional state at the time impacts how much they trust someone, even when that emotional state has nothing to do with the other person or the situation.": Jennifer R. Dunn and Maurice E. Schweitzer, "Feeling and Believing: The Influence of Emotion on Trust," *Journal of Applied Psychology*, 88, 2005, 736–748.

p. 93 "In one study, 78 teams of 3 to 4 undergraduate students each were tracked over 10 weeks.": Sheila Simsarian Webber, "Development of Cognitive and Affective Trust in Teams: A Longitudinal Study," *Small Group Research*, 39, No. 6, December 2008, 746–769.

p. 93 "Just after World War II, Leon Festinger and his colleagues Stanley Schachter and Kurt Back conducted a classic social psychology experiment.": Leon Festinger, Stanley Schachter, and Kurt Back, *Social Pressures in Informal Groups: A Study of Human Factors in Housing*, Palo Alto, CA: Stanford University Press, 1950; Leon Festinger, Stanley Schachter, and Kurt Back, "The Spatial Ecology of Group Formation," *Social Pressure in Informal Groups*, eds. Leon Festinger, Stanley Schachter, and Kurt Back, Palo Alto, CA: Stanford University Press, 1983, Chapter 4.

p. 94 "Additionally, recent research has shown that the relationship between familiarity and liking goes both ways—liking can increase our perception of familiarity, and familiarity can increase our perception of liking.": Michele Williams, "In Whom We Trust: Group Membership as an Affective Context for Trust Development," *Academy of Management Review*, 26, 2001, 377–396.

p. 94 "Some research has shown that familiarity with a company from presence in the media was negatively associated with reputation ratings (regardless of whether the media exposure was positive or negative).": Roger C. Mayer, James H. Davis, and F. David Schoorman, "An Integrative Model of Organizational Trust," *The Academy of Management Review*, 20, No. 3, July 1995, 709–734.

p. 94 "Margaret E. Brooks and Scott Highhouse review research that supports the idea that greater familiarity with a company is associated with mixed emotions and ambivalence about a company.": Scott Highhouse, Margaret E. Brooks, and J. Yugo, "Role of Warm-Glow Heuristic in Corporate Reputations," paper presented at the Annual Conference of the Society for Judgment and Decision Making, Toronto, 2005.

Chapter 7

p. 99   "There's a fascinating book called *The Five Love Languages* by Gary Chapman.":
Gary Chapman, *The Five Love Languages*, Chicago: Northfield Publishing, 2010.

p. 108   "My favorite resource for generating unique content is a book by Mark Levy,
Accidental Genius: Using Writing to Generate Your Best Ideas, Insight, and Content.": Mark
Levy, *Accidental Genius: Using Writing to Generate Your Best Ideas, Insight, and Content*,
San Francisco: Berrett-Koehler Publishers, 2010.

Chapter 8

p. 121   "The authors of *Primal Leadership*, Daniel Goleman, Richard Boyatzis, and Annie
McKee, describe how leaders' emotions resonate with others.": Daniel Goleman, Richard
E. Boyatzis, and Annie McKee, *Primal Leadership*, Boston: Harvard Business School Press,
2004.

p. 121   "Emotional contagion can be a subconscious or a conscious process.": Elaine
Hatfield, John T. Cacioppo, and Richard L. Rapson, *Emotional Contagion*, Cambridge,
UK: Cambridge University Press, 2004.

p. 122   "In this type of emotional contagion, greater displays of emotion do not necessarily lead to greater feelings of emotion; rather, people are influenced by their perceptions
of the authenticity of the emotion.": Thorsten Hennig-Thurau, Markus Groth, Michael
Paul, and Dwayne D. Gremler, "Are All Smiles Created Equal? How Emotional Contagion
and Emotional Labor Affect Service Relationships," *Journal of Marketing*, 70, No. 3, 2006,
58–73.

p. 122   "An interesting 2006 study published in the *Journal of Marketing* investigated just
how 'service with a smile' works.": S. Pugh Douglas, "Service with a Smile: Emotional
Contagion in the Service Encounter," *Academy of Management Journal*, 44, October 2001,
1018–1027.

p. 123   "One of the things that people look for is a genuine smile, also known as the
Duchenne smile, after the physician Guillaume Duchenne, who discovered the two differ-
ent types of smiles.": Guillaume Duchenne, *The Mechanism of Human Facial Expression*,
New York: Cambridge University Press, 1990, original work published 1862.

p. 123   "Alicia Grandey of The Pennsylvania State University set out to answer this ques-
tion.": Alicia A. Grandey, "When 'The Show Must Go On': Surface and Deep Acting as
Determinants of Emotional Exhaustion and Peer-Rated Service Delivery," *Academy of
Management Journal*, 46, February 2003, 86–96.

p. 132   "Educational psychologist Richard Mayer conducted an experiment in which
he asked two groups of students to perform computer programming problems.": Richard
Mayer, "Elaborate Techniques that Increase the Meaningfulness of Technical Text: An
Experimental Test of the Learning Strategy Hypothesis," *Journal of Educational Psychology*,
72, 1980, 77–84.

Chapter 9

p. 138   "In 1954, social psychologist Leon Festinger came up with social comparison theory,
which states that we evaluate ourselves by comparing ourselves to people who have similar

characteristics to our own.": Leon Festinger, "A Theory of Social Comparison Processes," *Human Relations*, 7, No. 2, 1954, 117–140.

p. 139 "Noted researcher on influence Robert Cialdini and his colleagues Noah Goldstein and Vladas Griskevicius set out to discover exactly how social proof and similarity work.": Noah J. Goldstein, Robert B. Cialdini, and Vladas Griskevicius, "A Room with a Viewpoint: Using Social Norms to Motivate Environmental Conservation in Hotels," *Journal of Consumer Research*, 35, No. 3, 2008, 472–482.

p. 153 "To test the impact of the park's signage, Robert Cialdini conducted an experiment similar to the hotel room study he cocreated, but with the goal of decreasing rather than increasing an environmentally friendly behavior.": Robert B. Cialdini, Linda J. Demaine, Brad J. Sagarin, Daniel W. Barrett, Kelton Rhoads, and Patricia L. Winter, "Managing Social Norms for Persuasive Impact," *Social Influence*, 1, 2006, 3–15.

Chapter 10

p. 157 "If you're like the people in a classic experiment by Dennis Regan, you would return the favor.": Dennis T. Regan, "Effects of a Favor and Liking on Compliance," *Journal of Experimental Social Psychology*, 7, 1971, 627–639.

p. 158 "Learn more about this principle of spiritual marketing with *The Attractor Factor* and the other great works of Dr. Joe Vitale.": Joe Vitale, *The Attractor Factor*, Hoboken, NJ: Wiley, 2008.

p. 159 "That said, a few things have been found to influence customer tipping behavior.": John S. Seiter and Harry Weger, Jr., "The Effect of Generalized Compliments, Sex of Server, and Size of Dining Party on Tipping Behavior in Restaurants," *Journal of Applied Social Psychology*, 40, No. 1, 2010, 1–12.

p. 160 "When servers gave each of their customers a small piece of candy with the check, they earned 3.3 percent more in tips.": David B. Strometz, Bruce Rind, Reed Fisher, and Michael Lynn, "Sweetening the Till—The Use of Candy to Increase Restaurant Tipping," *Journal of Applied Social Psychology*, 10, 2002, 348–361.

p. 162 "As I discuss in more detail in *The Confident Leader*, there are three essential types of motivation: (1) achievement, (2) power and leadership, and (3) affiliation or social motivation.": Larina Kase, *The Confident Leader*, New York: McGraw-Hill, 2008.

p. 163 "In an interesting article called "Dialogue Involvement as a Social Influence Technique," Polish researchers Dariusz Dolinski, Magdalena Nawrat, and Izabela Rudak describe how people are more likely to take desired action when a request is preceded by a casual dialogue rather than by a monologue.": Dariusz Dolinski, Magdalena Nawrat, and Izabela Rudak, "Dialogue Involvement as a Social Influence Technique," *Personality and Social Psychology Bulletin*, 27, No. 11, November 2001, 1395–1406.

p. 163 "In 1995, a group of researchers discovered that the reciprocity effect did not hold true if the person who bought you the soda was a friend.": Franklin J. Boster, Jose I. Rodriquez, Michael G. Cruz, and Linda Marshall, "The Relative Effectiveness of a Direct Request Message and a Pregiving Message on Friends and Strangers," *Communication Research*, 22, No. 4, August 1995, 475–484.

p. 164   "The lead or the most important part typically comes first. For example, on Yahoo! right now there is a story with the headline '8 Reasons Carbs Help You Lose Weight.'": Shine on Yahoo! Healthy Living, "8 Reasons Carbs Help You Lose Weight," http://shine .yahoo.com/channel/health/8–reasons–carbs–help–you–lose–weight–2442968/, accessed on January 27, 2011.

p. 167   "In his bestselling book *Book Yourself Solid*, Michael Port discusses how to create a funnel of giveaways and paid products and services to move people through a process beginning with free and moving up to your premium product or service.": Michael Port, *Book Yourself Solid*, Hoboken, NJ: Wiley, 2010.

p. 168   "In a 2010 study, researchers went into four restaurants (two were major franchises) and observed 360 dining parties ranging from 1 to 17 people.": John S. Seiter and Harry Weger, Jr., "The Effect of Generalized Compliments, Sex of Server, and Size of Dining Party on Tipping Behavior in Restaurants," *Journal of Applied Social Psychology*, 40, No. 1, 2010, 1–12.

p. 169   "In his groundbreaking book *Influence*, Robert Cialdini tells a funny and poignant story: Walking down a street one night, he was approached by a Boy Scout who asked if he'd like to buy a ticket to their circus that Saturday evening.": Robert B. Cialdini, *Influence: Science and Practice*, 5th ed., Upper Saddle River, NJ: Prentice Hall, 2008, 36.

p. 171   "Adam Smith once wrote, 'The sentiment which most immediately and directly prompts us to reward, is gratitude.'": Adam Smith, *The Theory of Moral Sentiments*, 6th ed., Oxford: Clarendon, 1976, 68; original work published 1790.

p. 171   "Michael McCullough and colleagues at the University of Miami propose that gratitude helps us determine benefits in situations, increases the likelihood that we'll behave in helpful ways in the future, and motivates us to help others.": Michael E. McCullough, Marcia B. Kimeldorf, and Adam D. Cohen, "An Adaptation for Altruism? The Social Causes, Social Effects, and Social Evolution of Gratitude," *Current Directions in Psychological Science*, 17, 2008, 281–284.

p. 171   "Researchers Monica Y. Bartlett and David DeSteno published a study in 2006 that showed that when people felt grateful toward someone, they helped that person more, even on a dry and boring task.": Monica Y. Bartlett and David DeSteno, "Gratitude and Prosocial Behavior: Helping When It Costs You," *Psychological Science*, 17, 2006, 319–325.

p. 172   "Jennifer R. Dunn and Maurice E. Schweitzer from the University of Pennsylvania conducted a study that found that gratitude created a higher level of trust toward a third party (who was not involved in the feeling of gratitude) than when people thought about a time in which they were angry, guilty, or proud.": Jennifer R. Dunn and Maurice E. Schweitzer, "Feeling and Believing: The Influence of Emotion on Trust," *Journal of Personality and Social Psychology* 88, No. 5, 736–748.

p. 172   "Ryan Goei and his colleagues conducted two experiments to see what really influences people to take action: favors, apologies, gratitude, or liking.": Ryan Goei, Anthony Roberto, Gary Meyer, and Kellie Carlyle, "The Effects of Favor and Apology on Compliance," *Communication Research*, 34, No. 6, December 2007, 575–595.

p. 176   "In the book *Marketing Lessons from the Grateful Dead* (a great read, especially if you're a Grateful Dead fan like I am), authors David Meerman Scott and Brian Halligan explain how the Grateful Dead gave back through benefit concerts for 20 years and then established the Rex Foundation as a nonprofit organization, which has granted $8.5 million to charities.": David Meerman Scott and Brian Halligan, *Marketing Lessons from the Grateful Dead*, Hoboken, NJ: Wiley, 2010.

Chapter 11

p. 178   "Sheena S. Iyengar of Columbia University and Mark R. Lepper of Stanford University conducted a study of jam shopping at an upscale grocery store in California.": Sheena S. Iyengar and Mark R. Lepper, "When Choice Is Demotivating: Can One Desire Too Much of a Good Thing?" *Journal of Personality and Social Psychology*, 79, No. 6, 2000, 995–1006.

p. 182   "There is an economic theory called *loss aversion* put forth by Amos Tversky and Daniel Kahneman that shows that people strongly prefer to avoid losing money over the potential of gaining money.": Daniel Kahneman and Amos Tversky, "Prospect Theory: An Analysis of Decision under Risk," *Econometrica*, 47, 1979, 263–291.

p. 185   "A study cited in Twitter Power 2.0 by Joel Comm found that the best way to influence people to take action to follow you on Twitter is with the statement…": Joel Comm, *Twitter Power 2.0: How to Dominate Your Market One Tweet at a Time*, Hoboken, NJ: Wiley, 2010.

p. 190   "Too many choices has also been shown to prevent people from taking out a loan and enrolling in a 401(k) plan.": Sheena S. Iyengar, Gur Huberman, and Wei Jiang, "How Much Choice Is Too Much: Determinants of Individual Contributions in 401(k) Retirement Plans," *Pension Design and Structure: New Lessons from Behavioral Finance*, eds. O.S. Mitchell and S. Utkus, Oxford: Oxford University Press, 2004, 83–95.

p. 190   "Sheena S. Iyengar of Columbia University's Graduate School of Business and Emir Kamenica of the University of Chicago's Graduate School of Business set out to further explore this concept.": Sheena S. Iyengar and Emir Kamenica, "Choice Overload and Simplicity Seeking," New York, manuscript, Columbia University, 2007; Gavan J. Fitzsimons and Baba Shiv, "Nonconscious and Contaminative Effects of Hypothetical Questions on Decision Making," *Journal of Consumer Research*, 28, No. 2, 2001, 224–238.

p. 191   "Alexander Chernev gave people an option of chocolates from either a set of 4 or a set of 16.": Alexander Chernev, "When More Is Less and Less Is More: The Role of Ideal Point Availability and Assortment in Consumer Choice," *Journal of Consumer Research*, 30, 2003, 170–183.

p. 192   "Research scientists William Hedgcock and Akshay R. Rao used functional magnetic resonance image (fMRI) scanning to study people's brain activity as they were engaged in a task in which they needed to choose between trade-offs.": William Hedgcock and Akshay R. Rao, "Trade-Off Aversion as an Explanation for the Attraction Effect: A Functional Magnetic Imaging Study," *Journal of Marketing Research*, 46, No. 1, February 2009, 1–13.

p. 194   "One interesting study found that the way that information is given impacts behavior, even if the information is presented in the form of a hypothetical question.": Emir Kamenica, "Contextual Inference in Markets: On the Informational Content of Product Lines," *American Economic Review*, 98, No. 5, 2008, 2127–2149.

Chapter 12

p. 199 "Benjamin Franklin said of his process for making decisions...": Nathan Goodman, *A Benjamin Franklin Reader*, New York: Crowell, 1971.

p. 200 "Researchers Timothy D. Wilson and Jonathan W. Schooler were curious if over-analysis was linked with unhappiness.": Timothy D. Wilson and Jonathan W. Schooler, "Thinking Too Much: Introspection Can Reduce the Quality of Preferences and Decisions," *Journal of Personality and Social Psychology*, 60, No. 2, 1991, 181–192.

p. 201 "Timothy Wilson from the University of Virginia and Jonathan Schooler from the University of Pittsburgh and their team purchased five brands of strawberry jam ranked 1, 11, 24, 32, and 44 by *Consumer Reports*.": Timothy D. Wilson and Jonathan W. Schooler, "Thinking Too Much: Introspection Can Reduce the Quality of Preferences and Decisions," *Journal of Personality and Social Psychology*, 60, No. 2, 1991, 181–192.

p. 203 "An interesting finding in psychology research is that people make decisions differ-ently if the decision is a simple one versus a complex one.": Danielle Timmermans, "The Impact of Task Complexity on Information Use in Multi-Attribute Decision Making," *Journal of Behavioral Decision Making*, 6, 1993, 95–111.

p. 203 "A psychologist at The University of Amsterdam named Dijksterhuis observed peo-ple shopping for furniture at IKEA.": Ap Dijksterhuis and Zeger van Olden, "On the Benefits of Thinking Unconsciously: Unconscious Thought Increases Post-Choice Satisfaction," *Journal of Experimental Social Psychology*, 42, 2006, 627–631.

p. 203 "Dijksterhuis ran another study in which he observed people who had to make a decision about a less complex purchase: cooking accessories, such as can openers and vegetable peelers.": Ap Dijksterhuis, Maarten W. Bos, Loran F. Nordgren, and Rick B. van Baaren, "Complex Choices Better Made Unconsciously?" *Science*, 313, 2006, 760–761.

p. 204 "Research by Rebecca Hamilton and Debora Viana Thompson suggests that when evaluating a single product, helping people to focus on the process facilitates their choos-ing the more viable alternative.": Rebecca W. Hamilton and Debora Viana Thompson, "Is There a Substitute for Direct Experience? Comparing Consumers' Preferences after Direct and Indirect Product Experiences," *Journal of Consumer Research*, 34, 2007, 546–555.

p. 204 "In one study, students were given two scenarios about different apartments from which to choose.": Debora V. Thompson, Rebecca W. Hamilton, and Petia Petrova, "When Mental Simulation Hinders Behavior: The Effects of Process-Oriented Thinking on Decision Difficulty and Performance," *Journal of Consumer Research*, 36, No. 4, 2009, 562–575.

p. 208 "People decide differently when they have other things on their minds. Consider this study: Baba Shiv and Alexander Fedorikhin gave people numbers to memorize as they made their way to another room where they would repeat the numbers.": Baba Shiv and Alexander Fedorikhin, "Heart and Mind in Conflict: The Interplay of Affect and Cognition in Consumer Decision Making," *Journal of Consumer Research*, 26, 1999, 278–292.

INDEX

About the Author

Larina Kase, PsyD, MBA, is a licensed psychologist and sales and marketing strategist. Her clients include salespeople, coaches, consultants, psychologists, realtors, designers, financial professionals, attorneys, and other business owners who want to make marketing and selling less stressful and more authentic, enjoyable, and effective. The founder of PlatformBuildingCenter.com, she helps professionals position themselves as experts in their fields to reach more people through speaking, writing, media, and their Web presence. She is the author of *The Confident Leader*, coauthor of the *New York Times* bestseller *The Confident Speaker*, and author of the popular blog PsychologyofMarketing.com. Dr. Kase

regularly appears in magazines such as *Entrepreneur, Inc.*, and *Selling Power*, and on television shows such MTV's hit *MADE*, in which she appears as a communications coach. Larina greatly enjoys speaking about business growth strategies to audiences of entrepreneurs and professional service providers. Get Larina's e-course "Stand Out! Marketing That Grabs Attention and GetsResults" as a gift for visiting her at LarinaKase.com.